INTRODUCTION

by David Boyer

I COULD ALWAYS TELL. Limousines buzzed up and down the street. Grimy boys who typically favored ripped jeans and T-shirts glistened like grooms. Homely girls transformed themselves into neighborhood Miss Americas. Yup, prom night. And for one evening, our boring suburb resembled the ones I saw in the movies and on TV.

Initially, albeit misguidedly, I looked forward to mine; I even hijacked the prom committee senior year. Location, theme song, decorations, invitations, friends' dresses—I got involved in all the big decisions. Then I had to find a date.

My best friend growing up was a pretty, precocious girl named Julie. We met in kindergarten and, ignorant of the boy-meets-girl nature of prom, I grew more and more attached over the years to the idea that we would go together. Then Julie started dating Stu, the captain of the football team, and it became clear that she would be busy that night.

Without Julie, I watched in horror as, two by two, friends paired off. Not going was not an option; that in my mind was tantamount to coming out. Instead, I settled on Joanne, an orthodontically challenged junior that I met on the set of our high school's rendition of *West Side Story*. (Full disclosure: I also had braces at the time.)

It's been fifteen years since my prom, but I still remember much of the evening: the pre-party around a backyard swimming pool; comforting Joanne when she ripped the hem of her electric-blue satin dress; dirty dancing in a cramped late-night club in Manhattan. And then there was the limo ride home. Stretched out across my date's lap, I felt completely betrayed as the boy I pined for, the boy I fantasized about going with to the prom, made out clumsily with his date. Next to him, another friend rustled his hands beneath his girlfriend's wine-colored gown. None of this was lost on Joanne; she wove her fingers suggestively through mine, inviting me to make a move. I pretended to be asleep.

I sensed I was what my mother termed "AC/DC" long before prom night: I hung out mostly with girls starting in grade school; when I was ten, I joined a swim team and snuck peeks of the other boys as they suited up; around that time, I also began pilfering copies of *Playgirl* from the mall's bookstore. But in the back of that limo, the fantasy of prom and heterosexuality collided with the reality of being gay and closeted. And as much as I wanted to, I could not look away.

Growing up, I really thought there were no queers in my high school; there was no Gay-Straight Alliance, just an assortment of hallway rumors and drive-by insults. The only homosexuals I encountered were on daytime talk shows like *Donahue*, and most of them were cross-dressers. Like Tony Scalia, who graduated in 1979, I believed that because I was attracted to boys, I would grow up to be a transsexual too.

These days kids have plenty of queers to look up to and, not surprisingly, they're coming out earlier and earlier. Now they get to experience crushes, dating, breakups and puppy love while they're still puppies. Seth Meyer, a recent high school graduate from Long Island, even had to deal with something I'd never heard of: "over-acceptance." A month before his prom, he broke up with a cheating boyfriend, but worried that if he invited another guy they would become the center of attention from well-intentioned classmates. Figuring it would be more fun, he decided to go with his best female friend. "Ever since I came out, I've become 'the gay guy.' So everybody expected me to go with a guy," explains Seth. "The fact that I was going with a girl had a lot of people feeling almost like I'd betrayed them."

Seth's situation probably surprises gays and lesbians born before the Reagan years. We spent much of puberty covering up any hint of romance or sexuality, and we waited until college or later to come out. At that point, the last thing we wanted to think about was high school or prom night. But those memories are not easily purged. They may be boxed up and out of sight, but with minimal prodding, they emerge in all of their awkward glory. "It fades away and you don't even think about it," jokes Steffan Schlarb, class of 1988, "until somebody comes along and drags it back up."

To be honest, I cannot remember exactly what drew me back to the scene of the crime. But in 1997, fours years after I came out, I pitched a story to *Might* magazine for which I ended up interviewing nine gays and lesbians about their prom night. Even then the topic screamed book, but in 1997 I was younger and lazier. And at that point in gay history, a book about queers and prom seemed particularly esoteric— *Ellen* was still in the closet, Will hadn't met Grace, and gay marriage, well, that seemed like a battle for the next generation. Basically, there were bigger fish to fry.

But things change. As the gay rights movement was making progress in the real world and in Hollywood, I was learning quite a bit more about queer history. About gay life before the American Psychiatric Association dropped homosexuality from its list of disorders in 1973. About a time when it was illegal to cross-dress and you had to wear at least three garments conforming to your biological gender. Beyond Liberace and Rock Hudson, I discovered that Oscar Wilde, Virginia Woolf, Melissa Etheridge—even Mike Brady—were members of the tribe. During this period, I also revisited that *Might* article quite a few times; it still felt unfinished. On one of my daily subway rides between Brooklyn and Manhattan, eureka! I realized prom was the perfect vehicle for the gay-history primer I never had.

Even though many queers would happily skip the occasion, most do not. "Prom was like an obligation. If people didn't go . . . there was something wrong with them, you know?" explains Theresa Iorio, who graduated in the '50s. Not so ironically, prom shines a spotlight on coupling and romance, forcing queer teens to publicly confront an attraction that, until very recently, society basically condemned. How we have dealt with this rite of passage over the years suggests how being a gay teen has changed. That is also what this book is about.

For practically every American born in the twentieth century, prom is a point of reference. Though an American invention, "prom" is actually derived from the French word *promenade*, which translates to "taking a walk or stroll." According to etymologist Evan Morris, a.k.a. the Word Detective, when it appeared in English around 1570, "promenade" referred to walking back and forth in public to "display oneself or one's finery." By late nineteenth century it indicated a formal ball at a school or college; around this time "promenade" was also shortened to "prom." To this day, public displays of finery—be it a couture gown, a gorgeous date or a stretch SUV—remain an essential component of the ritual.

Proms, as we know them, began popping up in high school gyms at the turn of the last century and reached critical mass in the

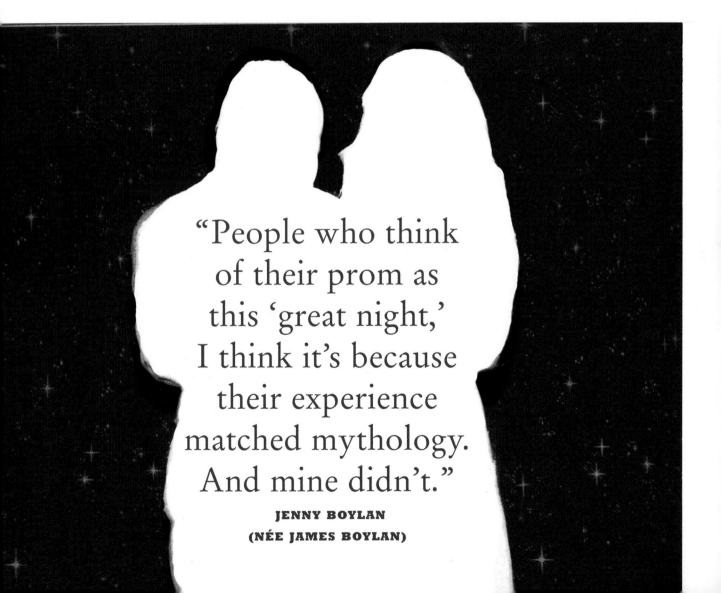

"People who think of their prom as this 'great night,' I think it's because their experience matched mythology. And mine didn't."

**JENNY BOYLAN
(NÉE JAMES BOYLAN)**

1930s, as more and more teens entered the public school system. World events (e.g., immigration and world wars) and domestic situations (e.g., industrialization and the Depression) fueled the surge in attendance. While less than one-third of high-school-age kids were enrolled in 1920, the ratio jumped to nearly one out of two in 1930, and roughly two out of three by 1940.

Sponsored by schools, proms were ostensibly a way to mark the end of the school year and the graduation of the senior class. But they've always had deeper significance. As more kids gathered in its hallways and the schoolyards, high school became a breeding ground for youth culture, a space where kids shared experiences and, for better and worse, influenced one another. Educators came to see it as their responsibility to guide and socialize teens before they became delinquents or dangerous.

Whereas other extracurricular activities like sports imparted the importance of physical fitness and teamwork, parents and schools took up prom as an opportunity to model proper adult behavior and courtship: boy asked girl; elegant invitations were sent out; etiquette was preached; and dance cards were printed. Teens voluntarily swapped youthful fashions for formal adult attire and danced to traditional orchestra music, the kind their parents favored. Although an idealized vision of heterosexual romance, for many, prom was a warm-up for their not-too-distant wedding day.

While some prom traditions—like corsages, invitations, and dressing up—remain unchanged, the rite has also always reflected the culture of the time. When Marinska Dolnar graduated in 1935, it was the heart of the Depression and her public high school, like many others throughout the country, cancelled prom because few people could afford it. "The word 'prom' wasn't a part of our

vocabulary," explains the Bronx native. "That was for rich people who lived on Park Avenue."

Proms became extremely popular in the years following World War II as America celebrated its political and economic ascendance. Around this time, Stumps, the nation's oldest purveyor of prom decorations and ephemera, introduced decorating theme kits, allowing the first of many generations to spend "An Evening in Paris" without leaving their school's gym.

Schools and proms were largely segregated until the 1954 Supreme Court decision rendered separate-but-equal education illegal. But widespread resistance to integration and civil rights movement lingered. Marc Scruggs, the only black kid in his high school in 1958, explains, "I knew what I had to do. That if I wanted to go to the prom, I had to find somebody from another town." So he "imported" a young black woman from another town. To this day segregated proms, though rare, are held in parts of the South.

As the counterculture blossomed in the late '60s and early '70s, proms became associated with the "establishment." In 1969, for instance, Avram Finkelstein ditched his prom in favor of protesting the Vietnam War. "It was the '60s. And a lot of people thought it was uncool to go to the prom . . . If you went to the prom, you were 'straight,' in the old sense."

As the country and its values swung to the right in the late '70s and the economy boomed in the '80s, prom became more attractive to teens who took their fashion cues from *Dynasty*, the rich-bitch soap that dominated ratings and came to signify the "decade of greed." At the same time, advertisers and teen magazines began to tempt and target teens more intensely, and proms became dramatically more elaborate and expensive.

No longer about mimicking adulthood, prom has become a celebration of youthful independence manifested in the form of stretch limos, belly-baring dresses, music choices (DJs not bands) and other brands of conspicuous consumption. For many, the actual prom is just an obligatory stop during a long weekend that includes pre-parties, after-parties and unchaperoned getaways. Parents and schools are still trying to exert some modicum of influence. "Our school . . . has the after-prom in the school gym just to avoid the whole, you know, drinking-after-prom thing," says Lynne James, a straight gal who proudly attended prom with

RIGHT ME AND MY DATE ON PROM NIGHT **NEXT PAGE** JANUARY 2004 HEADLINE FROM *NEW YORK TIMES*

a gay guy in 2003. "They try to really build it up as something that's fun to do; they bring in games like rock climbing and some kind of fun carnival-y stuff." Lynne and her date stayed for about an hour before declaring it lame and heading out.

During the 2003 prom season, *Newsweek* ran an article proclaiming same-sex prom couples "no big deal." But three months later, Amanda Blair and her female date were barred from their school's homecoming dance in rural Wyoming, the same state in which Matthew Shepard was gay-bashed to death.

While there are anecdotal reports of same-sex couples attending proms beginning in the late 1950s, the battle officially began in the spring of 1980, when Aaron Fricke sued his school's principal so he could attend his senior prom with Paul Guilbert. Aaron prevailed but faced vocal opposition from the public and many of his classmates, especially Dan Stewart. Says Dan, who became the first openly gay mayor in New York State, "I just wanted to lash out because I didn't want to be gay." So he aired his self-hatred on local TV and radio.

At the time, most teens were more like Lois Kasten, who appears on the cover with her date Patrick Mulhall. She was not out as a lesbian (even to herself) when she was crowned Prom Queen in 1980, but like many crafty queers, she was self-aware enough to escape the romantic vibe and sexual expectations of prom night by attending with a good friend who—surprise—turned out to be gay. The following year, the first gay prom was held in Boston. Since then, gay proms have become more and more commonplace. In fact, the first school-sanctioned gay prom took place in Los Angeles in 1994.

As the '90s wound down, couples at school proms began to reflect the growing acceptance of gays in America, especially in cities and on the coasts. Sociologist Amy Best notes in her book *Prom Night*, published in 2000, "The prom, an event that not only normalizes, but institutionalizes heterosexuality, has been taken up by gay and lesbian youth as a space to solidify their identity and contest heterosexuality as a taken-for-granted cultural practice."

That is also at the heart of the current debate over gay rights; queers continue to contest heterosexuals' lock on institutions like marriage and parenthood. And while Americans have proven they are okay with gays being their decorators and consultants on all things creative, we as a country are still grappling with how much is enough and what is too much.

These are ambiguous times. Not too long ago, having a queer eye for a straight guy was likely to land a person in the emergency room; now it can land you on the cover of *Vanity Fair*. At the same time, after the Supreme Court struck down antiquated and rarely enforced anti-sodomy laws, public acceptance of homosexuality, according to Gallup polling, plummeted to its lowest point since 1996. Just a few months later, when the Massachusetts Supreme Court ruled in favor of same-sex marriages, much of the initial discussion in the press focused on whom that decision might offend and how it could be overturned with a constitutional amendment legally defining "marriage" as a union between one man and one woman.

All of the progress made in the last decade seems to have riled the more conservative among us, who now seem intent on turning back

tropolitan area. $3.50

STRONG SUPPORT IS FOUND FOR BAN ON GAY MARRIAGE

IMPLICATIONS FOR '04 RACE

After Court Rulings, a Poll Sees Broad Unease on Same-Sex Relations

By KATHARINE Q. SEELYE and JANET ELDER

The latest New York Times/CBS

the clock. And, as history proves, progress is rarely linear: a few steps forward are often followed by a step or two back.

Who knows how queers will fare in this new millennium. Hopefully in a few years the stories that follow will feel like relics from a less-tolerant past. Still, it's worth knowing where we came from and how we got here.

In the introduction to *Working*, Studs Terkel's exploration of Americans at work, the legendary oral historian wrote, "I had a general idea of the kind of people I wanted to see, who in reflecting on their personal condition, would touch on the circumstances of their fellows."

While in no way a complete retelling of queer history, together, the words and photos of the men and women in this book capture what it's been like to be queer in the twentieth century and reflect the seismic shift in attitudes, not just towards sexuality, but also race, religion and gender. I am incredibly grateful to them for sharing their proms and lives with me. And now with you.

FRESHMEN

MANNY AND ANGEL, KING AND QUEEN
OF THE HARVEY MILK PROM IN 2003

ELLEN COMES OUT
1997

1992
BILL CLINTON ELECTED

1998
WILL & GRACE DEBUTS

With unprecedented speed, queers have gone from visible to acceptable, trendy to mainstream.

DALE STEWART WINS RIGHT TO ATTEND PROM IN DRAG
1999

2001
GAY PROM TREND REACHES FRONT-PAGE OF *NEW YORK TIMES*

SUPREME COURT STRIKES DOWN ANTI-SODOMY LAWS
2003

2003
FIRST PUBLIC GAY HIGH SCHOOL OPENS

THE VALEDICTORIAN

ARTHUR LARSEN

HARVEY MILK HIGH SCHOOL
NEW YORK, NEW YORK
CLASS OF **2003**

"Our honorary graduate was Hilary Swank," says Arthur Larsen, valedictorian of his class (wearing cap, on left). "It was really cool to have her marching with us; she put herself in there alphabetically."

Most schools cannot draw Academy Award winners to their commencement ceremony. But as many journalists and politicians, donors and detractors are quick to point out, Harvey Milk is not your typical high school.

In 1985, the Hetrick-Martin Institute started an alternative education program for queer teens and named it after Milk, the slain gay politician. It provided a safe learning environment for kids who had been harassed out of the New York public schools.

In the fall of 2003, having received $3.2 million from the NYC Department of Education to expand the program, Hetrick-Martin made front-page news when, amidst a few hundred supporters and a handful of protesters, it opened the new Harvey Milk High School, the world's first full-fledged public school for queer youth.

"I think this is historic," notes Arthur, an articulate poster-child for the school. "The city has acknowledged that we have young people who need more support. We're not in need of special education. Instead, the school prepared us for the real world with counseling and self-defense class."

I GREW UP IN BROOKLYN. I lived there until I was sixteen, then I moved to Manhattan. I didn't live with my family for a little while, so there was some distance there. But we're much closer now.

Originally, I went to the High School of Telecommunication Arts and Technology (HSTAT) in Bay Ridge, Brooklyn. I had a strong support system at HSTAT; my friends were mainly the drama kids that were, you know, in the drama classes and the drama club. But there was a lot of anxiety being one of the few gay kids out of 1,200 students. I had to change in the vice principal's office for gym, because the boys' locker room wasn't too keen on me

> ## "I came from this really academic school. And then I got there and it's a bunch of trannies vogueing."

being there, because they knew I was gay. I said to the administration, "You know, this is not going to be a comfortable situation for me. What should I do?" And that was their solution.

Ultimately, I just needed to be in a smaller environment. I kind of remember reading about the Harvey Milk School in an article. And my guidance counselor knew about it as well, because her daughter had applied. She got me all of the contact information about the school, and I called and I made my interview appointment. I was very on top of the people at Harvey to get in.

I remember my first day there. That was a scary moment, because I came from this really academic school. And then I got there and it's a bunch of trannies vogueing. And I'd never met a tranny before; I didn't know what that was. So that was a culture shock. I wanted out right away; I begged to be kicked out. And they wouldn't let me. They knew it

There's a lot of acceptance. But it's not so different from other high schools: there's pettiness, there's gossip, there's all of that.

There were also cliques, but they were very sexuality-aware. The transgendered girls hung out with the other transgendered girls who were in the drag ball scene; the pretty, gay, white club boys hung out together; the quieter, white lesbians hung out together. Then there was a group of us who were mixed and a little more mingled.

My best friend from Harvey was this girl Laura, she's actually a straight girl—like the only one there—and this kid Paul. And they were both a little more with me academically. And they had similar interests, you know, just music and the arts. I missed the friends that I had from my old school, but I think that's with any transition. And they were really great about my whole switcherooni. They came to volunteer at Harvey and they joined the after-school program. They even came to my prom!

Prom was this awe-inspiring moment: seeing all of these same-sex couples dancing together and feeling that was normative. You know, it didn't seem forced or out of the ordinary in that situation. It just sends this chill, this chill of happiness through you.

I actually went to two proms. Junior year, the prom was at a club that was donated. The theme was "Midnight" or "At Midnight" or something like that. The night was actually rather depressing because of the dating thing; I didn't date very much in high school. Occasionally, I would date, but nothing serious. I wound up taking a good friend and her girlfriend. Yeah, *that* was fun . . . to watch this really cute couple dancing all night as your date.

And then senior year I took Paul, because he had graduated already and he wanted to come back. Since I wasn't dating anyone, going with my best friend seemed like the next best thing. It was a fun night and, you know, it was my senior year, so it was just good to be with friends and be sociable.

was an adjustment and they knew I would do really well there. And they were absolutely right.

I think my story is a little unique from the kids at Harvey: before I went there, I was still attending school regularly and my academics were a little bit stronger. And a lot of my classmates had just given up on school before they went to Harvey.

The academic part was frustrating for me at first, because the classes were not as rigorous as I was used to. But, to make up for that, they allowed me a lot of independent study. And they just encouraged me just to do what I do best—whatever that was at the moment, they encouraged it. Like for one semester I did teaching assisting within the school for a class on gay and lesbian literature. Part of my job as a T.A. was to help outline the curriculum with the teacher. And part of my final assignment was actually to teach three classes.

The teachers made sure I was very aware of my potential. When I handed in work, they graded it at the level I was able to perform at. Some people want to say the school is easy because a lot of the other kids don't perform as highly as I do. It wasn't. Because the teachers knew I could hand in an A+ paper and therefore would only take that from me.

Harvey is definitely different than other schools, because individuality is encouraged to no end; that's a big part of being there. There's a lot of acceptance. But in many ways, it's not so different from other high schools: there's pettiness, there's gossip, there's all of that. There's a lot of harshness, because when you receive nothing but hate all of these years and all of your life, you just sort of know to give that back.

ABOVE A HALLWAY IN THE NEW HARVEY MILK HIGH SCHOOL
RIGHT HEADLINE FROM THE *NEW YORK POST* AND IMAGES FROM
THE FIRST DAY OF SCHOOL, 2003

said.

Arthur Larsen, who graduated from the program last month as valedictorian, is thrilled with its expansion into a full-fledged school. "I'm now an alumnus of a real school!" he said. "There's going to be more students. In four years, I want to work here."

GOD HATES FAGS

MATT IS IN HELL

THANK GOD FOR Sept. 11

YOU'RE OUR ROLE MODE

MILK HIGH

POLICE LINE DO NOT CROSS

NEW YORK POST

CITY FINAL

25 CENT

www.nypost.com

GAY HIGH

w city school a first

Welcome to Harvey Milk High lage — the nation's first full-fled exclusively to gay kids. The NYC open in the fall with 100 students.

Prom was this awe-inspiring moment: seeing all of these same-sex couples dancing together.

In terms of dress, they always try to encourage more of an elegant, traditional prom. But this is Harvey Milk, so people do their own thing; people did come in leather pants, and people did come in capes. The first year, I had this outfit made—this amazing gold, black and copper outfit. Custom made. With a top hat. It was amazing. The second year, I dressed down a little bit with sort of a club outfit.

And we had a Prom King and Queen. My year, we decided only the seniors could run. And then you just went up to the table during prom and put your vote in. I think it was more of a popularity contest. Angel was the Queen and Manny was the King at my senior prom; Angel is transgendered and Manny is a gay boy. He struggled for a while; his attendance was really bad. So actually for him to win it was really sort of a great moment.

Graduation was like two or three days after prom. It meant a lot to me to be the valedictorian; it sort of affirmed all the work I put into going there and being there. It was nerve-wracking, but I really loved my speech. I was nervous because I knew it wasn't your typical valedictory speech. I could have given a speech about "how lucky we are" and "go forth" and "yea!" Instead, I talked about the divisions and the need for unity. We're cast in these roles of, you know, the gays hate the dykes, the this hates the that. And it's like, why are we doing that? The goal is unified, why can't the actions be? It was received really well; I got a standing ovation.

And my father was there and my stepmother, and they were really proud of it. They were tearful actually. This was sort of new for them, to be in this room with all of these queer people. None of these people are like me, you know? And my father and stepmother were used to me, but I'm a very specific type of person. I don't think I come across in many ways—at least I don't think I do. It was awesome the way they responded; it was a really big moment for them. And me, too.

But the most amazing moment, I think, was at the graduation lunch. Barry Diller donated this big lunch at this restaurant that he owns, and we went and we just celebrated. It was a great feeling sitting with all of these people who came so far, and we all had a big sigh of relief that finally we were done. And we had those Henri Bendel gift bags—they were also donated.

You know, I'm not gonna lie, we got a lot of gifts. And maybe that was because we were a

OPPOSITE TOP ARTHUR AND FRIENDS AT THE JUNIOR PROM **OPPOSITE BOTTOM** AT THE SENIOR PROM **ABOVE** ARTHUR PALS AROUND WITH NEW FRIENDS IN COLLEGE **LEFT** AT GRADUATION

Arthur's involvement in the Harvey Milk School's transition from private program to public school was minimal. "I did a lot of interviews and I spoke at a lot of different things to sort of show that Harvey is a reputable program," explains Arthur, who is now at SUNY Purchase double majoring in Sociology and Women's Studies. "I think the media attention hurt things and it helped things. I think now the school is under a microscope; they can't make any wrong moves or everyone will be on top of them. Because I think a lot of people are waiting for it to fail."

"And the teachers are not playing around anymore," he adds. "They used to be more lenient. Now, homework is due when homework is due. It's definitely a much more seriously run school."

Arthur is proud of how far his alma mater has come—more than doubling in size this year—and he's optimistic about its future. "I think it's going to continue to expand. I know they plan on having 175 kids next fall. And expanding the school is a good thing so long as they still provide appropriate emotional support."

"I also think it will become just an integrated, great school," he says. "I don't think it's always going to be this big queer school; soon acceptance will rise and it's going to become a much more diverse school."

Arthur remains in touch with classmates and is working with the school's administration to launch an alumni association. As for next year's prom, "I'll go if I am invited either by someone attending the prom or as a chaperone. I'm sure the school is apt to have me come back."

small school that didn't get the money the Board of Education had given to everyone else. I have Dolce & Gabbana sunglasses; I have all of these Levi's and Marc Jacobs clothes—stuff I'd spend tons of money on if I could—and I paid nothing for it. It's not like Thursday was Calvin Klein giveaway day; it was more event-organized. They'd make gift bags and they were given out in relation to Christmas or in relation to graduation.

I don't think donations are going to stop now that it's a public school, because there are so many great people in this community who want to give back. I think the adult queer community wants to make sure our generation and this next generation succeeds. And they're going to back that up. And that's spectacular.

No matter what stage the school is in, I am just glad to have been a part of it. If I hadn't gone to Harvey Milk, I think I would have finished high school. Grudgingly. But I'd probably be in some community college somewhere just barely getting through classes. And it's shaped what I want to do with my life: I've decided that this is a community I want to be a part of; this is the community I want to work in.

LYNNE JAMES*

SYCAMORE HIGH SCHOOL
SYCAMORE, MISSOURI
CLASS OF **2003**

Five years ago, her family relocated from a small, rural town (population 1,900) to a slightly larger one (population 12,000) where most people work in farming or the auto industry, and churches outnumber bars two-to-one. The initial response: why are you here?

"This town is so much built on family names; being new and not having any relatives here makes you a little bit of an outcast. And anyone overly creative, overly loud is kind of looked down upon, too," says Lynne, a self-described artistic theater girl, who, in the end, directed the most risque production ever mounted in town: a family-friendly version of *Les Miserables.*

"I kind of floated until senior year," admits the brassy, fair-skinned brunette, who stands out among the school's flock of tanned, blonde clones. "I had really casual, conversational relationships, but no real deep friendships." Then she met Nealle, a closeted gay boy with an obsession for Cher. And her eventual prom date.

* names and locations altered to ensure Nealle's anonymity

THE FAIRY PRINCESS

WE MET IN THIRD-YEAR SPANISH. We didn't really notice each other for the first several weeks. Then one day I was passing out Tic Tacs. I offered one to Nealle, and he seemed kind of bored, so I started talking to him. I casually mentioned those Tic Tac commercials where somebody breathes into their hand and then, you know, tries to determine if they have bad breath. I said, "That's not possible." So we both tried it—to breathe fast and sniff fast—and we looked like complete idiots. And over that funny, little incident a friendship formed. And pretty soon the seating arrangement switched, and we were next to each other and we talked a lot and, um, he eventually told me he was gay.

We'd known each other a couple weeks when he told me. I still remember this: I was looking for a three-hole punch for something. I asked him if he had one, and he said, "Do you think I carry one around in my pocket?" And I said,"You know, they have those cute little ones that you put in your binder." And he was like, "Cute little three-hole punch? Don't make me gayer than I already am!" I think I kind of smiled at him and changed the course of the conversation, but we shot each other a look that was like, Okay, I understand you.

We didn't really talk about it again until we started spending our lunch hours together. We'd huddle in this little corner of a hallway, which was the only place that was warm in the entire school, and talk. It felt kind of good,

I've learned to embrace it, but I found alternative names, like "fruit tart" and "fairy princess," because "fag hag" really isn't my favorite.

because it was somebody who was different from everybody else I knew. And it was kind of intriguing; I don't mean that in kind of like a sick curiosity way, but, you know, I wanted to learn more about him and who he was.

Nealle's family's lived here, I believe, all his life. And I think it would be harder to be more established in the community and have something that you're trying to hide or that you feel that you need to hide. His family doesn't know, and I don't know how they'd react. When Nealle and I started hanging out, I actually told my parents he's gay. I just wanted them to know, because obviously it wasn't a romantic thing, and I didn't want them to think that it was. And they were just kinda like, "Oh." But they didn't push it aside like, "You can't hang out with him."

Now that we're friends, I kinda notice some of the little whispers like, "He must be gay." And he knows about it, too. If you're a little too active in drama or you're a little too stylish in your clothes or you pick out the wrong shoes, you run the risk of being called gay. And that's a horrible thing. Sophomore year I actually had those whispers about me. Like, "Why isn't she going out with anybody? Doesn't she want to go out with anybody? Well, what's wrong with her?" If I really cared what people thought, it might be hurtful or it might feel awkward, but I really don't.

I never really had a desire to be really close to any guy here. And as an independent, strong-willed woman, you don't exactly have a line at your front door of guys wanting to date you. Or ask you to prom.

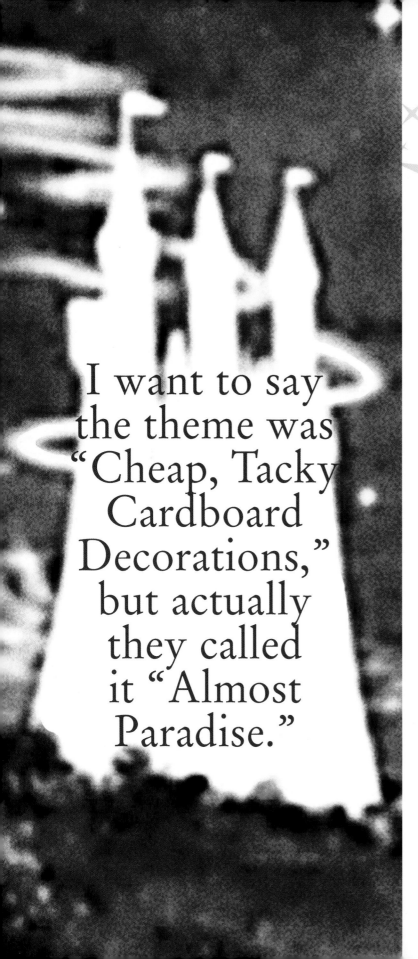

I want to say the theme was "Cheap, Tacky Cardboard Decorations," but actually they called it "Almost Paradise."

In my school, prom is open to both juniors and seniors. I did not go junior year, and when people asked why, I was like "I'll go my senior year"—not really knowing if I would. I talked to Nealle a little bit about it during the winter, you know, just kind of casually. At the time, I'd told him, "Oh, I don't know if I wanna do a formal this year. I haven't even done one yet in my high school career and I'm not too crazy about it." So I kind of gave him the idea that I really didn't even wanna go.

Months started to pass and prom talk grew heavier and heavier around school. But I decided I kind of wanted to go, because it's, you know, that special senior-year memory. Soon other well-meaning senior girls were trying to set me up with various males. One girl was determined to find every single senior a date so that everybody could go to the prom. Oh, God—it was just overbearing! And the only person in the world I really wanted to go to the prom with was Nealle, because we're good friends. And it's free of the sexual tensions and free of having to try to make up casual conversation with somebody you may not know all that well or have the desire to know all that well.

I kind of avoided the subject with him. So, finally we were on the phone one night, and I just kind of casually brought up, "Oh, you know, do you have any prom plans?" And he said, "No. Do you want to go with me?" And I just about screamed "YES!"

I had another guy friend, whose mom is a beautician, reserve a hair spot for me. I already had a red satin dress that I absolutely loved. I did my own nails and had my hair done and did my own makeup. And, you know, usually it's this huge group of girls that are going together and they all huddle in each other's houses and . . . I was alone in my bathroom. I had my music on, doing my makeup, and, you know, waiting for him to come to the door.

He rang the doorbell, and I came running down the steps to greet him. And we did pictures in the living room, and we did pictures in the family room. Then we had to go do pictures outside. And while we were doing pictures outside, we saw the neighbors peeking out around their doors. You know, they all wanted to see. It was like, "Oh, there's Lynne going to prom. Oh yeah, it's senior year. Well, who is that guy? He's really cute."

Then we drove over to his house and we did pictures there. His parents knew we were just friends, but of course mom was there and grandma was there and older sister was there. And it was all that, "Oh, I just love your dress, and your hair looks so nice! Oh, stand together in front of the fireplace! This will make such a good picture." All the typical prom stuff.

None of the hotels in Sycamore have banquet halls or anything like that, so prom was at a local restaurant that has what they call the Evergreen Room. I want to say the theme was "Cheap Tacky Cardboard Decorations," but actually they called it "Almost Paradise." They had some palm tree stuff up and at the door they were selling the Hawaiian leis that were imported from Hawaii. And everybody got all decked out for prom night. Now, in a town like this, "decked out" means different things to different people: you had some neon-blue suits for the guys; you had some very, very badly fitting dresses for the girls. So we spent the night whispering catty comments and drinking bad punch and dancing in each other's arms; we actually stayed for almost the whole prom.

Our school also has the after-prom in the gym just to avoid the whole drinking-after-prom thing. They try to really build it up as something that's fun to do; they bring in games like rock climbing and some kind of fun carnival-y stuff. And it's the big thing for all the couples to buy matching outfits and come to the after-prom together. So, we went over to my house to change: we just did tennis shoes, and he had denim shorts and I had denim capris, and we had matching black T-shirts from the show *The Producers* that had "When you got it, flaunt it" across the front; we thought that that was just too perfect! We signed in and got some free, school-provided cheap Mardi Gras beads and played a couple of the games. We got our pictures taken and then we said, "Okay. This kind of stinks."

So we skipped out and went to this little twenty-four-hour diner on the edge of town; it's next to a truck stop. I think it was like three in the morning, and we're sitting there eating biscuits and gravy, and there's, like, all these truckers. And our waitress comes up to us and she said, "Well you two match!" And we just cracked up. Then he drove me home and he walked me to my door. He hugged me good night, and that was the end of my prom.

I'm glad I experienced it once and I'm glad that I won't be, you know, the girl who grows up saying, "Well, I never went to prom." But once was enough.

It's funny, it kind of occurred to me when we were dancing that every little girl dreams of prom, and it's this fabulous Cinderella moment. And mine was like *My Best Friend's Wedding*. You know, you end the night dancing with the gay guy. And in the end, I wouldn't have it any other way.

So what is the attraction to gay men? "You have the male presence and it's not as cutthroat as having a girlfriend—you know, girlfriend in the friendship sense," explains Lynne. "I've yet to meet a gay man who hasn't faced some sort of rejection. So they're usually a lot more comfortable with the emotional side and they're more sensitive to your feelings."

Lynne never thought of herself as a fag hag until a friend in Indianapolis suggested it. "I've learned to kind of embrace it," she says. "In the past, it probably connoted somebody who couldn't find a boyfriend. Now it's just somebody who wants to have a meaningful friendship with a guy who happens to be gay. I think it's become more accepted; just turn on *Will & Grace*."

Still, she's found some alternates for the label, "like 'fruit tart and fairy princess,' because 'fag hag' really isn't my favorite."

Lynne is aware it's not all good times and Cher. "Sometimes you find yourself looking for someone for the fag that you hag instead of being busy looking for a guy for yourself," notes Lynne, whose ideal man is "somebody who's a very creative person and really likes music and theater."

Like it or not, there's probably a lot more fags in this hag's future, now that she's matriculated at a large state university that is approximately twenty percent queer. And Nealle, currently a senior at Sycamore, is only forty-five minutes away.

"He's not right next door anymore, but we're still only a phone call away," says Lynne. "So, we can still, you know, talk 'til one a.m."

w: Connie and me in prom attire.

THE PROM KING

KRYSTAL BENNETT

FERNDALE SENIOR HIGH SCHOOL
FERNDALE, WASHINGTON
CLASS OF **2001**

During the final month of her senior year, Krystal Bennett found herself at the center of a controversy. It began in her rural town, near the Canadian border, when her classmates elected her Prom King. Then it became a national news story.

Make no mistake, Krystal was already a budding activist. The only openly gay student in a school of nearly 1,500, Krystal successfully lobbied the administration to add queer books to the library's shelves. And while she knows it sometimes turned off her classmates, "when somebody would say something that I didn't appreciate or found offensive, I didn't hesitate to tell them that I found it offensive and ask them not to say it anymore."

This courageous spirit runs in her family. "My mother and sister never did anything really vocal or out there, but it was just the way that they never stepped down or gave in. I knew that no matter what I did, even if the entire school hated me, I had them. And that's what I needed."

Still, when Krystal and her girlfriend, Connie, pulled up to the prom, they had no idea how memorable their night would be.

WE WEREN'T EVEN PLANNING ON GOING. Freshman year I vowed never to go to any high-school-affiliated anything. I went to my junior prom, and that was like the only dance I ever went to. I went to only one football game, which is like a sin here. But it got to the point where I was like, "Okay, this is my last opportunity to do anything school-affiliated, so I might as well go and have fun with it and not take it too seriously."

> "I had joked around with people about, 'Yeah, I'm going to wear a dress.' Nobody's ever seen me in a dress."

My dad said he would give me the money to go if I wanted to. And so I went and got a tux, and Connie went and got a dress.

I went to the Men's Wearhouse, which was interesting. There was one lady there who was really sweet and totally willing to help. But then there were others who were giving me that look like, "What are you thinking?"

I think the last time I wore a dress was to my grandmother's or my grandmother's sister's funeral, when I was in fifth grade. Oh no, I lied; I wore a dress to my mom's wedding, only because she made me. That was two years ago. I hated it; I cried. I told her I was not going to wear it. But I knew that it would just break her heart if I didn't, so I wore it. But it's just embarrassing. So there was no way I was wearing a dress to the prom. I had joked around with people about, "Yeah, I'm going to wear a dress." Nobody's ever seen me in a dress.

There really wasn't much of a reaction when we showed up to the prom. Some of my friends were like, "Oh, hey, that looks really good." But everybody expected it. I've been open about being gay, and I had worn a tux the year before to junior prom.

It looked like a room filled with Backstreet Boys and Britney Spearses.

The prom was held at a place called the Majestic, which is—I want to say it looks like a big ballroom-type area—it's just a huge, open, wood-floored room with pillars. It was really dark, and they had strobe lights and lasers. The prom theme was Shangri-La. So they had red and gold pieces of cloth wrapped around the pillars. They had a little fishbowl with Chinese fighting fish on a table when you walked in, and out to the side there were tables with snacks and drinks on them. It was not a very big space for as many people as there were, so it was kind of crammed.

It looked like a room filled with Backstreet Boys and Britney Spearses. It was terrible. A couple friends of mine—two girls—didn't have boyfriends, so they were just like, "Let's go together." And they dressed up in '80s prom dresses. So they were there together just joking around. It was nice not to be the only two girls there together, even if they weren't there *together* together; it threw some of the pressure off.

When we first walked in the door, they handed out a little piece of paper that said "King" and "Queen." And you wrote down the names of the people that you thought should win. I was joking around with a friend, and she said, "I voted for Mr. Vandriot," who is the school resource officer. And I said, "Man, you should have voted for me; I want to win." And she was like, "That'd be awesome." So the few people around me voted for me—like my best friends. And I'm not sure how it spread.

So we were just hanging out, dancing, just goofing around. We were getting ready to leave and we were walking toward the door and they said they were going to announce the winners. So we figured, Well, we'll hang out a few minutes and see who wins.

And we were all like, "It's going to be Kara Johnson and Joey Joshua." Joey is a half-African-American, half-Caucasian football player, basketball player, athlete, big, goofy guy. Kara is like a five-foot, two-inch Barbie doll who's the head cheerleader.

the girl who would be king

... like me to fit in **during**

... trying. **by Krystal Bennett**

Above left: My girlfriend, Connie, and me last year. Above: High school graduation.

...ere must be something about me to ...gh about. When one friend got out ... car, she giggled and asked me not ...k at her butt. I felt humiliated.

...use me, sir

...hat summer, and I missed my ...espite their reaction. I was ...ecoming an outcast at the ...o I played the "boyfriend" ...ut rumors started anyway.

...bout

...d me out.

...I thought all I had to do was tell my close friends that I was gay, and deny the stories. But the worst rumors are the ones that are true—you can't fight them. The truth spread all over the school. I couldn't lie about being

...one night ab... ...loved me ...atter what ...totally freaked ...d sai... out. But being ...tracted to girls felt right inside, too. I ...didn't talk about it or tell anyone. I had ...boyfriends until I was about 15 years ...(I'm 18 now). I'd meet a guy in

...past Van ...Dyke... ...ered to steal the street sign for me. They laughed about it. But to me, they were laughing at the

So they said, "The 2001 Prom Queen is Kara Johnson." And we're like, "Okay, whoopee, big surprise." And I didn't hear them say my name, so I'm just standing there, because it was totally not something that I expected; and I figured even if I got enough votes to win, just on principle, the school would not let me have it. But they did, which surprised me a lot.

Knowing the teachers in charge of it, I'm sure that there was definitely, "Is this a mean joke? Do we think Krystal will appreciate this? Should we throw this out?" And I think that they were all pretty much aware that it was something that I would not have been offended by or found a bad thing. I'm not comfortable in a dress, and I definitely did not want roses and a tiara; it just wasn't going to happen. It's me: I have a shaved head, I shop in the boys section, I consider myself borderline transgendered. So if the "excuse me, sir" in the grocery store doesn't bother me, why would this?

> ## "Concerned" community members began calling the high school and saying, "How could you allow this?"

After I realized they were talking about me, I went up there and Kara put her arm around me for the cheesy picture. Everybody was yelling. My friends were like, "Yea!" and I got high-fives from a few people; it was pretty cool. There were some people that just stared, and there were some people who were definitely disgusted.

At the time, I was involved with the local PFLAG chapter. And the co-chair of PFLAG here is a very media-obsessed person. She asked me if it would be okay if she wrote an e-mail and bragged to all of her friends. You know, "Our little Krystal did this." And I was like, "Yeah, whatever. Not a big deal."

I wasn't thinking that she was going to be sending it to newspaper people. And they were like, Oh, I can do a story on this. So I got a call from the *Bellingham Herald*, which is the local paper. I'm figuring section D, column fifty; nobody'll see it. Instead it was page

one, which was really shocking to me, because that's really kind of personal.

At first I thought it was really cool, because it was just a few little things. And then a teacher of mine attacked me in front of the class and was like, "How dare you? You have no right. You're publicly embarrassing this school." She just went off on me, and that really ticked me off. So I decided that I should do more media.

I got a call from a TV station in Seattle and then another station in Seattle and then the *Seattle Times* and then just tons of different media.

Kudos for publishing prom king story

Several weeks back, a very negative letter about gay, lesbian, bisexual and transgendered people appeared in The [...] and I sent an inquiry to the editorial board asking about what their guidelines were for including such an un-Christian-like diatribe. Having received a much appreciated response from the editorial page editor, I realized what I already knew — that there are many different viewpoints, and each person is entitled to their own opinion, even if it denigrates an entire co-culture of society.

Therefore, my opinion is, "Way to go Krystal Bennett!" Thank you for the courage to honor your true self, just the way God made you. May you continue to find people on your path who will support you as you make these tremendous strides in educating people about diversity and inclusiveness.

Thank you to The Bellingham Herald for putting this wonderful news on the front page. I have absolutely no doubt in my mind that you will receive many negative letters and calls about your decision to publish this story at all, much less on the front page. So kudos to you. You have published stories on the front page that I have cringed at in the past, but that i[...] goes bac[...] to the f[...] that

You know, the *Today* show and *Good Morning America* and *Seventeen* magazine. *YM* magazine called me, and they were like, "We want you in our prom issue next year." And I'm thinking, Yeah, me in there with Tyra Banks. I'm not seeing that one happening.

Then "concerned" community members began calling the high school and saying, "What happened? How could you allow this?" And the local conservative radio station had its telephone lines open for discussion on this issue, which meant that every conservative Republican in Whatcom County was calling to talk about how I was a disgrace and how I pollute the public school system. It was like forty-eight hours of live-radio bashing me. And the opinion pages in the newspapers were going crazy.

A Congressman even made some remarks about how I was the reason they should have school prayer in schools. I made Congressional discussion; that to me is insane. At that point, I was an eighteen-year-old kid just trying to graduate school and make a difference to the people around me and educate some people.

It was terrible. It was embarrassing. I would go to the grocery store and, you know, like in the old movies about the civil rights movement, where the black woman walks into the store and the mother grabs her child's hand and scurries away? People were literally doing that.

A lot of students that I never expected to say a word to me said, "Oh my gosh Krystal, that was so awesome. You're so brave." And then a lot of students who I thought were really cool never spoke to me again. Never looked me in the face. Never. Nothing.

It became really awkward to go to school. I had teachers vocally sharing their opinions on the situation. Like, I had a teacher telling a group of students, "Well, if Krystal wants to be gay that's fine. But she should never have been Prom King, because she's not a guy."

The prom thing didn't start out as an activist position or a political statement, it was simply that I wasn't comfortable being a queen, and king fit my gender position better. And who doesn't want to win? Every kid wants that popularity stance and to look back in forty years and say, "I was the Prom King." It wasn't about putting it in anybody's face.

I actually just got a package today in the mail from the woman who help me write the story for *Seventeen*, and there were like fifteen letters that were sent in to the editor. Fifteen letters of girls saying, "Oh, you know, it was so amazing, and it gave me the courage to come out" or "Only two people at school knew I was gay, and this article made me want to tell ten more."

I recently spoke at Gay Pride in Seattle, which was scary. I've won a scholarship; I've won two awards—just things that I never would have gotten in my life without doing all of this. It's a really neat feeling, because you step back and you're like, Wow, I didn't even mean to do that. Like, I got that just for waking up that day and being who I am.

POSTSCRIPT

After the controversy died down, Krystal's life continued to change. She broke up with her girlfriend, moved in with her sister. "And I'm actually in the process of transitioning," she explains, referring to her decision to shift from female to male, from Krystal to Krys.

Having been on hormones for almost a year, Krys's voice has deepened and he has begun to grow facial and body hair.

"All my friends from high school have been really open-minded. I ran into someone who I hadn't talked to since the day I graduated, and she was like, 'Oh, I'm so proud of you.' My mom is really the only one in my family who's not supportive of my transition," says Krys. "And she's not *not* supportive, she just doesn't think that I'm old enough. She thinks that if I wait longer then I'll know for sure."

"But I was never really a girl," says Krys. "I was nominated Prom King because I was always way more masculine. I mean, I always kind of knew that I was off. I automatically thought it was being gay. It was when I was a junior in high school that I realized, Okay, there's a word for what I am, there are steps to take to fix it.

While Krys has not been politically active since the transition began, he and a trans friend have been talking with a community leader about starting a trans youth group. "When we were lesbians it was easier to find somewhere to go," explains Krys. "Once you're trans, you don't fit in with the gay guys or the lesbians—it's definitely a third-wheel kind of situation."

THE JESUS
FREAKED

CARLA NATHAN

SOUTH HIGH SCHOOL
MINNEAPOLIS, MINNESOTA
CLASS OF **1997**

She was vice president of the student government; she threw shot put for her school's track and field team; and as a totally out lesbian, she was voted runner-up for Homecoming Queen. Still, coming out was a nightmare.

Her peers and school weren't the problem. In fact, South was one of the first public schools in the country to train teachers about LGBT issues and create safe spaces for queer kids. Carla's problem was a homophobic and increasingly religious mother unwilling to accept her daughter's sexuality.

"Some people are like, 'My parents are going to kill me.' And that's what kids say. But, no, my parents really were going to kill me," explains Carla, who later became a youth counselor and sexuality educator, in part, because of her difficult coming out.

IN JUNIOR HIGH, KIDS GET TO PICK which high school they want to be in. Even then, South was known as 'the gay school.' And I think deep down I knew that I was gay, but I wasn't that conscious about it yet. So I think I chose it partly because it was my neighborhood school, partly because all of my friends were going there, and I think unconsciously I knew, yeah, it was a different kind of school.

> "I really understood the few cues that my parents gave me: that it wasn't okay to be gay, not with them, not with their kid."

One of my favorite moments at South was when a friend of mine, her girlfriend had cheated on her or something. And we're walking down the hallway—we were probably skipping class to be honest—and it's like me, the captain of the wrestling team and a football player. And my friend, she's totally crying, and one of the guys is just like, "It's alright. You're gonna find somebody else; she wasn't good enough for you anyways." And it's the kid from the football team saying this. And that's the kind of random school it was.

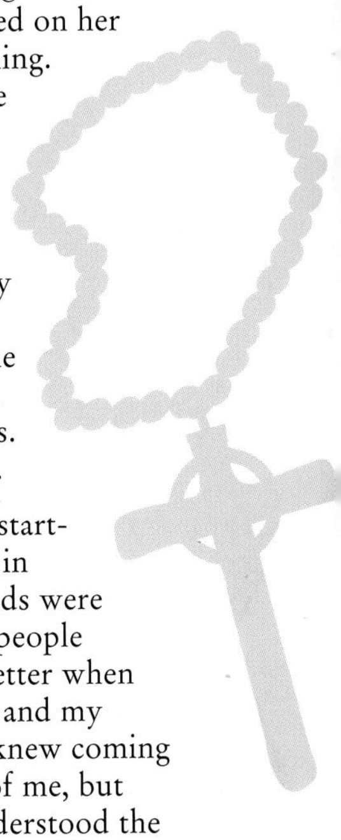

Sophomore year was when most of us were starting to come out. I was going back and forth in terms of coming out to myself, and my friends were kind of helping me along the way. So many people said, "Dude, you're going to feel so much better when you come out"—you know, teachers, adults and my friends. I was super, super depressed, and I knew coming out was going to take this huge burden off of me, but I was worried about my parents. I really understood the few cues that my parents gave me: that it wasn't okay to be gay, not with them, not with their kid.

My mom started praying, "Lord, please let the devil out of my child." She was basically performing an exorcism.

I know some people think kids these days have a lot easier time coming out. And I believe in some of that. But when my friends and I were coming out, talk shows and Jerry Springer were at their height. And I swear it seemed like every damn time I came home, my mom was watching talk shows, and there was negative or crazy stuff on about gay folks. And I'm like, This is not helping my situation.

I do remember a couple of times—and this is when I was starting to become more comfortable with where I was at—she would say stuff, and I would challenge her. And one day, she was like, "Why do you care? Are you gay?" And I totally freaked out and I was like, "Uh, no, not so much."

That was probably my sophomore year. Around that time, my dad had a stroke and almost died. And I remember being out to myself at that time, but was just like, There's no way in hell, with everything that's going on, that I can tell them.

After my dad's stroke, they became more religious; so that didn't help either. My mom started to do weird things: She wouldn't give me messages from my gay friends and she was saying, "You can't spend the night at anyone's house." She started becoming really controlling about what I wore and being like, "I think you need to grow your hair out." I think she kind of figured out I was gay and was pretty much thinking she could fix it.

A little bit after my eighteenth birthday, I came out to them. My mom just flipped. We were in a family therapy session; the therapist dude didn't know what to do. She was just going off. And then she calmed down and left like everything was fine.

We just didn't talk about it, like nothing happened. A couple of days go by and I came home one night, and as soon as my mom hears me beep the car alarm, she is outside and she's rubbing some oil on the door knob and praying. She basically had her pastor pray over oil—like you can do it with olive oil—to make blessing oil.

I came inside. She grabbed my head and put some on my forehead and started praying like, "Lord, please let the devil out of my child." And I'm like, "What the hell?" My mom was basically performing an exorcism. And my dad, after his stroke, just wasn't his normal self; sometimes he's like a five-year old. So, he's on the couch, just flipping channels while this is happening. And my mom has like the big, five-inch, family bible with pages marked off. And she starts reading some passage aloud, and I'm screaming like, "Stop! Don't do this!" And she had me sit down on the couch, put some more oil on my head, and had me read some stuff aloud.

She had also gone through my stuff and found a *Lavender*, which is a local LGBT magazine. (The bad thing is that there's tons of porn and phone-sex lines in the back, but there's good articles, too; I mean, it's the gay newspaper, so it has a little bit of everything.) And she's like, "Is this what they're teaching you in school?" And I was crying and screaming, "Do you want me to leave?"

A couple of weeks earlier, one of my friends' parents told me I could come live with them, because they knew stuff was just not good at home. So I called them from school the next day, and they said, "You can totally move in."

I can kind of laugh about it now, but that night I had to look at my room and think, If I can never come back here, what do I want with me? I was able to get ahold of my birth certificate. And I packed a bag with my favorite clothes

and some of my CDs and my school books and that kind of stuff. And I packed a couple boxes and hid them in my closet. That Sunday, while my parents were at church, my friend's parents picked up my stuff and I moved into their house.

I didn't leave my parents a note—I didn't even think about that—and they totally freaked out. My mom showed up at school the next morning and came to my class. We went out to the courtyard, got in an argument, and she started hitting me. Open hand, closed hand, on my face and on my chest. I didn't even hit her back, which to me is still amazing because I had been taking self-defense class and Tae Kwon Do for two-and-a-half years. But because it was her, I was just immobilized.

I was totally embarrassed because my friends could hear everything. And also because, for any other kids that either weren't out or had issues with gay folks, it was that thing of like, "That's what happens."

I actually had to go to the ER because my chest was swollen and I couldn't breathe. They gave me Vicodin and some other stuff to make the swelling and the pain go away. My mom wound up getting arrested and had to spend the night in jail. And I had to get a restraining order.

Prom was in May, so not quite a month later. And I was like, "I'll be damned if I'm not gonna go to prom." I still had a job, so I had money. And I had met this older black lesbian at an event, which was like a godsend. I mean, all through coming out—Minnesota's like a pretty white state—I'm like, "There aren't any gay black people." And I felt even more isolated in that respect, because I didn't have any adult role models.

She and her partner totally took me under their wing, and they helped me go shopping and stuff for prom. I wanted to wear a tux—there was never a question of me wearing a dress—and

We had two gay tables because there were so many of us. It rocked!

here we have the Mall of America, so we just went there and I wound up buying a suit. It was kind of weird, because it was just a guy's store. But I was determined.

I went to the prom with this girl in my English class, this girl named Sari. She was out as bi at the time, and she totally had a crush on me and kept asking me to go. But she's one of those people that you know just ain't right. But I'm a lesbian and I'm kind of butch, and she had a nice body, you know, so I was like, "Alright." And, I mean, we were friends or associates or whatever.

My other friends that were out—some of them were dating people, so they were obviously gonna go with their girlfriends. And then some just went with other girls that we were all friends with. There was probably about ten or twelve of us—all gay, except maybe one girl—in butch/femme combinations.

Sari came over to my friend's parents' house where I was still staying. And my lesbian role-model person was front and center, and she helped me get ready and took a bunch of pictures. And then we went to prom.

First, we went out to dinner to this kind of alternative place. And people were pretty cool—cuz it was girls in tuxes, girls in dresses, I mean, you could tell we were going to prom. And the restaurant happened to be a couple of storefronts down from this lesbian bookstore Amazon. We went in there because I wanted a gay earring, and the cashier was like, "Oh my God, that's so cute; you're all going to prom. Oh my God, I so wish I could have done that when I was your guys' age." And we were like, "Will you take a group picture of us?" So we took a group picture, and then she took a picture with us. And then some random person walking down the street took a picture with all of us. And then we went to prom.

Prom was at the Radisson. We got there and, yeah, there were some people who were like, "What the hell?" But I remember the really funny thing was that boys that I didn't even know came up to me—because the style of my suit was pretty new—and all of them were like, "Oh my God, where did you get that? I was looking for a suit like that." They were just like, "Oh my God, your suit is so nice." I got mad compliments that night.

And you know at prom how they always—whatever the theme is—they have the cheesy statue that everybody takes their picture under? We totally did that in the couples that we came with. We all danced in our couples. We sat at a table; we had two gay tables because there were so many of us. And that was prom. It rocked! Oh, and then the other thing is that District 202, the queer youth place here, has a gay prom every year. So then we all went to that the next night. And I think I went with the same date.

It was totally different. At our school prom, we didn't do a Prom King and Queen, but at the gay prom they did. So the Prom Queen is usually a little, cute gay boy, and the Prom King is like a butch lesbian. And there were opposite-sex couples and same-sex couples. And it was at a hotel in downtown Minneapolis. And there were like a couple hundred kids. And that totally rocked, too.

I had no contact with my parents that weekend. And I think that was one of those times that I was totally just not thinking about them. I mean, I don't even think they know I went to prom.

THE
GIRLJOCK

SUMMER LEE

ARAGON HIGH SCHOOL
SAN MATEO, CALIFORNIA
CLASS OF **1993**

"I went with my boyfriend at the time. He was always pressuring me to have sex, and I almost lost my virginity that night," Summer remembers about her junior prom.

"But I totally just didn't feel moved by him and I knew you were supposed to feel something more. So I faked starting my period!" explains the former student-athlete who attended Stanford University on a softball scholarship. "Before that I kind of thought it might be him, but after that I was like, Okay, maybe it's not him. Maybe it's me."

A few months later, she came out. "I happened to go to a café, and a bunch of dykes were there smoking. One of them winked at me, and I wanted to faint. The friend I was with—who's straight—looked at me and was like, 'Are you gay?' And I'm like, 'Oh my God, yeah.' And she's like, 'My dad's gay.'"

Summer wasn't particularly shocked; after all, she grew up in a suburb of San Francisco.

I HAD THIS WHOLE CEREMONY WITH MY FRIENDS of sitting them down, one by one, at this café and saying, "I need to tell you something." I was really afraid that some of them would reject me. Thankfully they didn't; in fact, three out of four said, "I suspected." And they were all really supportive.

I was still afraid that people on my team, if they knew I was gay, would blackball me or treat me differently. And when you're on a team, you're on a team—there's no running away; there's no escape. So I only told two of my friends on the team.

> "The worst thing you can be as a woman in sports is a lesbian. There's a lot of straight fear of 'the lavender menace.'"

I think the worst thing you can be as a woman in sports is a lesbian. There's a lot of that straight fear of "the lavender menace" that goes on. In fact when I was growing up and getting ready to go to college, there were these suburban myths; like this one girl went to some Texas school and she came back because the coach was lesbian and the players were lesbian and they were sexually harassing her. I think that was utter bullshit. But that was the controlling image of lesbians in sports.

And I definitely think there's some overcompensating with makeup and hair; there's this huge push for women to play sports and still be feminine. It's almost like you have to bargain with society like, "Okay, I'm gonna play sports, but I'll still be feminine so you can let me." I totally felt that pressure.

At my school, there was also a lot of pressure to fit into a certain mold and dress a certain way, kind of preppy. And before I came out I fit that mold: I had long hair, but not too much

I ended up cutting a lot of my hair off right before coming out. And when I came out, I cut off even more.

ABOVE SUMMER WITH FRIENDS AND GRANDMA
BELOW SENIOR PICTURE RIGHT AT BAT FOR STANFORD
PREVIOUS PAGES SUMMER WITH HER DATE TODD AT
WINTER FORMAL; AND IN SECOND GRADE

makeup; you didn't want to be too slutty. I ended up cutting a lot of my hair off right before coming out. And when I came out, I cut off even more. Plus, the girlfriend I was dating at the time was very militant and dykey. And so, I started wearing combat boots—before I was wearing little loafers.

So that was really noticeable to people. But nobody really said anything, except once in a while these guys that nobody liked would say, "Oh, are you a San Francisco dyke?" But they were kind of on the margins of our high school anyway, so everybody was like "Whatever?" And I would just laugh or say, "Fuck you."

I never really gave it too much thought, but clearly some of the adults noticed something was going on, too. My sister, who is two years younger, was called into the office at my high school by a school counselor—she was this busybody lady—and she's like, "What's going on with your sister? Is she gay?" And my sister is pretty evolved and she was like, "Why are you asking me? Ask her!" So then the counselor called me in and was like, "Summer, is

there anything going on in your life that you want to talk about?" And I was like, "I'm fine. Thanks. Ba-bye."

The other thing related to school is that I was able to use my coming out as sort of an excuse for things; because I was a 4.0 student, and my senior year I wasn't doing as well. I ended up getting two Bs or something. And one of my teachers saw me drinking a beer in Menlo Park with one of my new gay friends and I'm underage. So the next day at school, she was like, "I saw you drinking in public and I am appalled; you're senior class president and it's See Red, Say No Week." (That was Barbara Bush's thing; she thought that if we saw red, we would "say no" to drugs; everybody was supposed to wear red or put red posters up.) I had nothing to say to my teacher but, "I'm gay." And she was like, "Oh, honey," and gave me this big hug. She was hugging me so hard I was choking; so she thought I was crying.

I don't think there was a lot of homophobia in my school as much as it was "don't be so different," or "don't be too butch." But I think I always felt different—and not just sexuality wise; I'm also half Asian—but I was never able to embrace it. And finally, here was something that forced me to come to terms with being different. It was kind of a relief. I think I had some fear of losing my status or, I don't know, of not being perfect, but then I also found a lot of freedom in not being perfect.

Coming out absolutely represented something cool to me. There were a lot of chic, cutting-edge things going on in the lesbian community in San Francisco. And there was definitely the appeal of playing against what's expected and yet still getting to do it—still getting to be senior class president and go to Stanford. And I think this is probably unique to the Bay Area: there was a sense that you could be gay and not be the total stereotype. If I had come out in Utah and I had to go to a fucked up country-western bar with a bunch of haggard, old ladies, I probably wouldn't have had an easy time coming out. I would have thought, That's not me. I'm not coming out. That would have been too far of a leap for me. I could leap a little bit, but I couldn't jump across a huge river to become this totally different person.

It was already a leap for me to have these gay friends that were so different than the friends I had in my normal, mainstream, high-school life. All my gay friends were kind of mod and depressive; half of them were high-school dropouts, some of them may have graduated from high school, but they definitely weren't going to go to college. And they weren't very ambitious; I mean, they were ambitious about the next girl bar. And my friends from school were all Ivy League-bound with 4.0s and involved in extracurricular activities and knew what they wanted to be when they grew up and, you know, were very preppy.

Because I was having this other life, I started to not be as involved in campus life. But it was complicated. At our high school we have a winter formal, which I think was just as important as prom. And

I needed to go because, as class president, I had organized it. And my girlfriend didn't want to go; she dropped out of high school, so she was not gung-ho about any high school-sponsored event. Period. So, I picked Todd Hoffman—the gayest guy in school—as my date. But it was hard, because she hated men. She did not even trust this flaming gay guy. Eventually I think she met him and was like, "Okay, you can go with him."

I think that's why I didn't go to my senior prom. It was like, I'm not going to go through this negotiation process anymore. My friends kind of wanted me to go with my girlfriend, because they wanted to see everybody's reaction. There probably would have been a lot of whispering; nobody would ever do anything directly to me. And I don't know if it's because they would never say it to "Summer Lee," or they just didn't have the balls to say it to anybody. I don't know.

And actually the hugest thing that happened that still kind of disappoints me is . . . I think there were five of us nominated for Prom Queen; and one of my best friends missed the list and knew she was number six. So she found

My friends wanted me to go with my girlfriend, because they wanted to see everybody's reaction.

LEFT SUMMER WITH BASKETBALL TEAMMATES AT THE SCHOOL'S WINTER FORMAL
ABOVE WITH HER PARTNER AT THEIR COMMITMENT CEREMONY IN 2001

out that I was faltering about going and she definitely pressured me to not go. So then I said, "Well if I don't go, I still think I should keep the nomination." And it was almost like I didn't give a fuck about the nomination, but I felt like she was kind of knocking the legs out from under me. And that's what happened: after I announced that I wasn't going, she pushed something through so that I lost the nomination and she could be nominated. I was pissed off at her for a while and then I was like, "Fuck it. Why should I care about being Prom Queen?" She did apologize later and, you know, we're like family—things happen.

Frankly, I was a little surprised that I was even nominated. And I think I was nominated because people wanted to hold onto the old me. On paper, I did all of the things you were still supposed to do; it's just that I had been doing something a little different of late.

For a minute, my girlfriend and I were gonna go to the prom. We even talked about what we were going to wear—"Should we do the drag thing or what?"—but I think it came down to that there was a good girl party, G-spot, going on that night and, because I went to a bougie high school, prom tickets were like 180 dollars for a couple or something really outrageous. I also sensed that she was too freaked out about prom to have fun with it.

So we went to G-spot instead. It was really happening: it was a young, hip crowd. To me, this was where "lesbian chic" was coming out of at the time. Even the music was cutting edge. I mean, they're still playing "Push It," that stupid Salt-N-Pepa song. But it was cool then.

I remember being there and saying, "Okay ladies, this is my prom night." You know, I mean obviously nothing at G-Spot was going to resemble the prom, but I remember telling people, "Okay, this is my prom night. Let's have fun and let's all get along," because I was in a group of particularly dyke-drama people. And I remember drinking more than I usually do just to say "it was my prom." There was some of that "fuck prom, fuck them—this is where I'm at." But I think that was a front for deeper feelings of sentimentality about losing something that was precious. And my friends from high school were pretty disappointed, too. I think it was a signal that we were all changing away from each other a little bit. And it wasn't going to be the same.

POSTSCRIPT

After waiting in line for eight rainy hours, she and her partner wed as San Francisco issued same-sex marriage certificates in 2004.

Summer remains close to her friends from high school. "At the time, I was probably reacting against what I had been before, and kind of going more to the extreme and being more militant than I think is my nature," she admits. "As I started to even out, they could identify with me more. But there was always a sense of unconditional love. Thank God."

As their tenth-year reunion approached, Summer's self-confidence was a tad wobbly. "If you graduated in the top two-percent of my high school, then you should have gone off and done amazing things," she explains. "And financially I'm pretty well off because my partner makes good money. But somehow that doesn't even matter."

Still, her sense of humor remains intact: "I just cut off all my hair, and then I got the reunion thing in the mail, and I was like, *Whoops*. Because I had really short hair my senior year, and they're probably going to think I'm not more complex than I was when I left."

Instead of scaling the corporate ladder after graduating Stanford, Summer spent the last decade working within the domestic violence movement, helping mentally ill adults, traveling and realizing that grad school was not for her. "Now I play golf on a women's golf team."

Sadly, attitudes about lesbians in women's sports haven't evolved much. "Nobody on my team will talk to me about being gay. Everybody asks questions, but they ask around me. They can talk about their husbands, but I can't talk about my partner. It's so tired."

SOPHOMORES

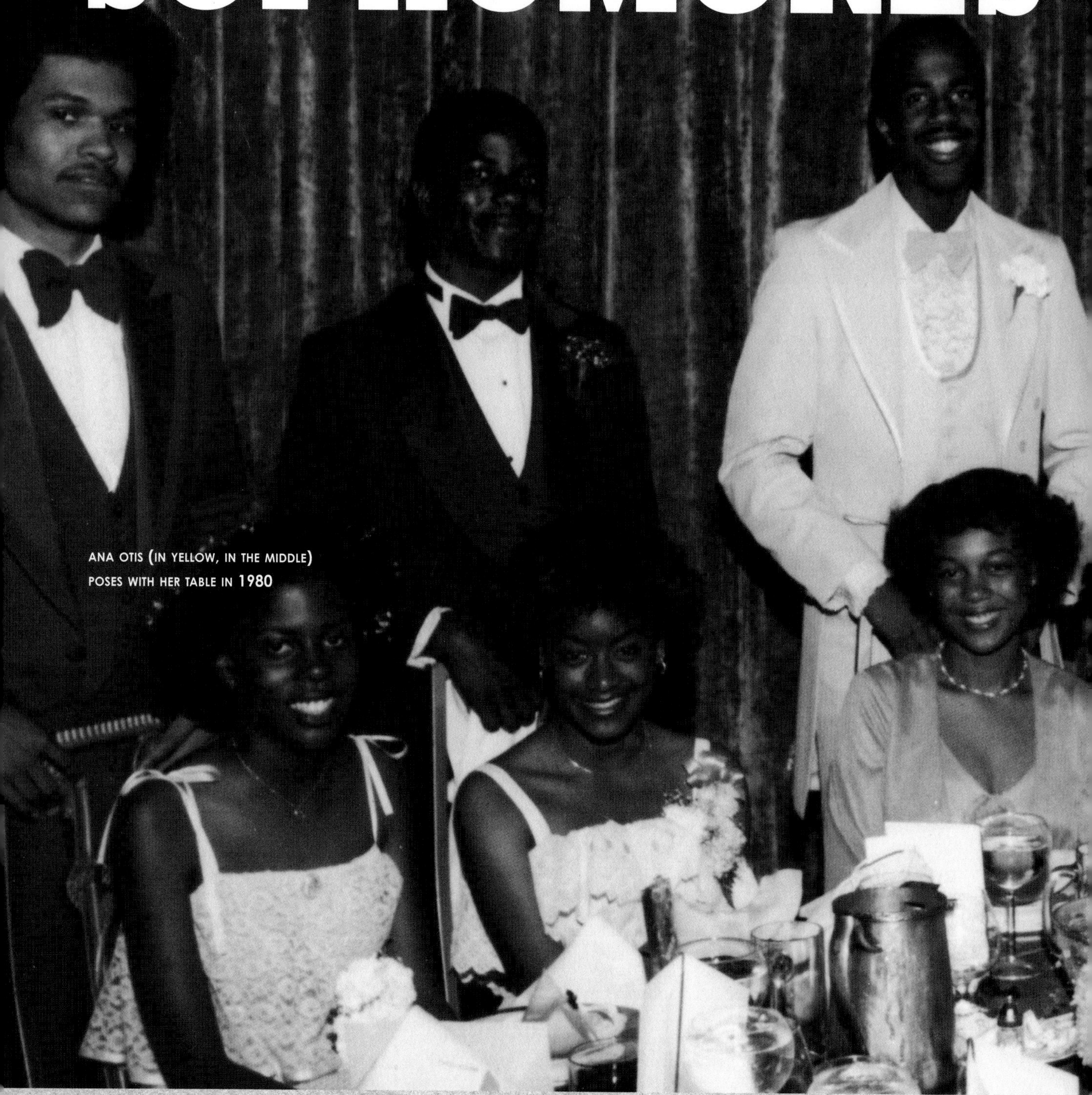

ANA OTIS (IN YELLOW, IN THE MIDDLE)
POSES WITH HER TABLE IN 1980

FIRST GAY PROM HELD IN BOSTON

WISCONSIN PASSES
FIRST GAY RIGHTS BILL

CENTER FOR DISEASE CONTROL
INVESTIGATES A "GAY PLAGUE"

1981   1981   1982

1980   1982

AARON FRICKE WINS LAWSUIT AND ATTENDS PROM WITH PAUL GUILBERT   FIRST GAY GAMES HELD

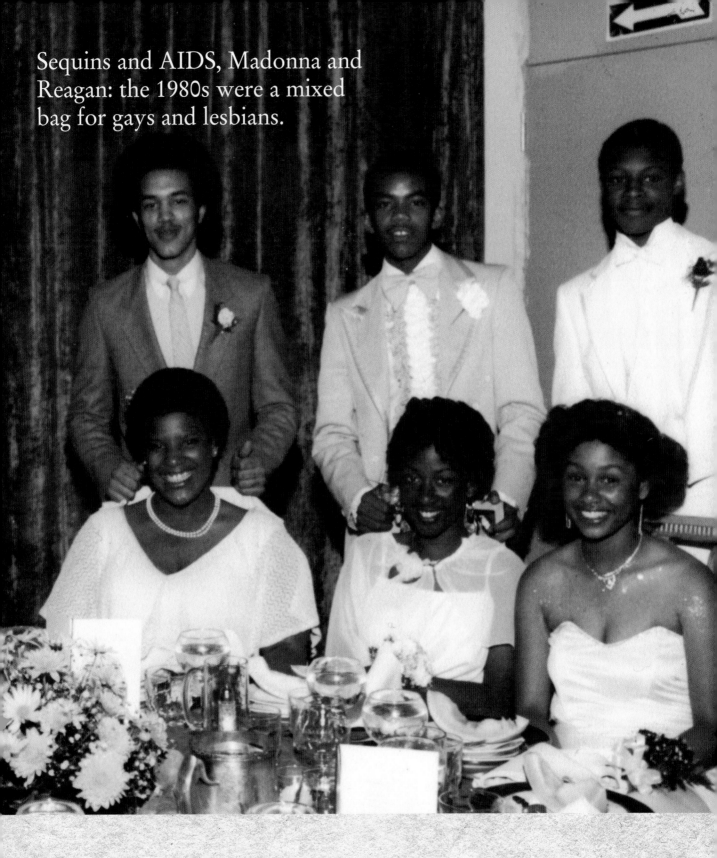

Sequins and AIDS, Madonna and Reagan: the 1980s were a mixed bag for gays and lesbians.

THE HAPLESS
ROMANTIC

STEFFAN SCHLARB

ST. JOSEPH'S PREPARATORY SCHOOL
PHILADELPHIA, PENNSYLVANIA
CLASS OF **1988**

Unlike many gays and lesbians who dread the ritual, Steffan looked forward to his prom. "My parents are Baby Boomers and I had seen their prom pictures," he explains "I knew that eventually I was going to get to go and it was going to be something really cool."

Prom, in young Steffan's dreams, was to be a pivotal evening in his dreary high school career: he would bring a sassy date who would give him "dude cred"; they would be named King and Queen of the Prom; and, after the dance, they would retire to a hotel and he would (finally!) lose his virginity.

"During the '80s, there were all those teen sex movies. There was *Porky's* and *Sixteen Candles*; they all reinforced what prom was supposed to be about," says Steffan. "That it was a life-changing experience. And it was something you would remember forever and ever and ever."

And he does. His memories, however, are funny in the darkest sense. And the photo, well, you be the judge.

I ALWAYS KNEW that prom was the shit. It was basically what your entire school life—and life up to that point—was leading to. That was your shining moment. And if I didn't go, it would lead me down a path of being a loser, basically alone for the rest of my life.

> "In retrospect, I think I was looking for a *Pretty in Pink* kind of prom. And that really didn't happen."

What I thought would be the ideal night is: I would be with a bunch of friends and we would rent a limo, and we'd all get into the limo and party. We'd stand up in the moon roof, driving down the streets screaming. We'd arrive at the prom and we'd run in and push everybody out of the way and dance. And then somebody would spike the punch. Streamers would be flowing. Just laughing and singing and dancing. Then we'd blow out of there and go to a hotel room, and I'd have sex with my amorphous date. It didn't matter who she was; I just knew that I would have sex. After we had sex, we would go out and party again. And I would have immediately morphed into a man.

Of course, we'd have our pictures taken. And it would be one of those things where my mom would have it on the mantel, a picture of me at the prom. People would come in and say, "Oh, they look so great together . . . what a beautiful date you had . . . you were so well dressed." Stuff like that. And it would last in my memory and I would keep the picture on *my* mantel until I was dead.

Well, it didn't go that way.

There was a lot of pressure in school among people, you know, like, "Who are you taking to the prom?" Because we went to an all-boys school, nobody really knew who people were bringing. And I just knew it was getting close to the time and I needed to have a date.

She came down the stairs and I didn't even recognize her. Her hair was Aqua Netted up like a bear trap.

I really didn't identify with anybody in my school; it was religious and conservative and very jock oriented. I was not jock oriented. I tried out for every fucking team I could—one embarrassment after the other, hopes raised and then dashed.

Because I didn't make it on any teams, I would just hang out at the train station after school and read comic books. And all of these kids would hang out there; I guess it was because there were lots of us from the suburbs who went to private schools in the city. That was kind of my social scene during high school.

I ended up meeting this girl there. I don't even remember her name—that tells you how important it was. She was really smart. She went to a good school in the city and I just liked her style. She was Korean and she had her hair off to one side, kind of in a bob, almost shoulder length, and it hung down over her eyes. She wore black-framed glasses, smoked cigarettes and wore a big, plaid men's jacket.

I don't know how long I knew her—maybe just a few weeks. But prom was coming up, so I decided to ask her. She was definitely flustered; I suspect that she just never thought that this casual hanging-out thing would result in going to somebody's prom. But she said yes. So I was like, "Great."

I was kind of psyched, because I knew that she was the right type of girl. I guess I had figured out my own myth about what the prom was about. Because I knew I wasn't going to have a bombshell, I was going to do it a different way; it was going to be this cool girl, and we were going to have a cool time.

And so prom night: I took my dad's car. My dad had this really cheesy car; it was a Chrysler LeBaron convertible. Totally ridiculous car, but it just made sense. I went and picked up my friend Greg, then we had to pick up my date.

I arrived at her house, and I kind of expected her to wear a black slip dress or something kind of tough or something that just fit who I knew her as. I guess, in my head, I thought she'd be wearing the men's sport jacket and the black glasses and everything; I thought she'd just put a dress on. When I got there, it was a much different scenario.

I knocked on the door. Her parents opened it and there's, like, her entire extended family. Tons of people—cousins, uncles, etc.—all speaking Korean. I'm standing there waiting, and she

TOP WITH MOTHER AND BROTHER, 1978 **ABOVE** STEFFAN'S ALWAYS BEEN A FAN OF HALLOWEEN **RIGHT** ART INSPIRED BY A TEEN CLASSIC **PREVIOUS PAGES** STEFFAN WITH DATE ON HIS BIG NIGHT

pretty in pink

was kind of brought out to me, which I guess is another prom stereotype. But I just didn't expect it from her.

She came down the stairs and I didn't even recognize her. Her hair was Aqua Netted up like a bear trap or something. It just came up, with these wings that went up into the air; it was like a death flower. The bangs were just shellacked up into nothing and then on the sides up into nothing, but kind of curling, like a bun. And then she had more hair that came down and curled under. But it was all the consistency of plastic, shiny plastic. And she was wearing this really traditional white satin prom dress with gloves; she just looked miserable.

Immediately, I was like, "We have to get out of here." Because it was an awful situation. Her family was there to see who was taking her to the prom. I guess they had expectations. I have no idea what they thought of me because they were all speaking Korean. I think I remember they were really nice . . . and I had gotten a corsage for

God, it was such a disappointment. The pictures didn't even turn out good.

her. It's weird: here I was expecting her to play out a different arm of my fantasy, but I was still following the other fantasy.

So we got into the car. There was no acknowledgement at all about what had just happened. It was totally awkward and weird. She was obviously nervous; we were all kind of nervous.

We got to the prom, and, like, proms suck. You sit and have to eat bad food, you know, "Chicken or beef?" I mean it's basically like being on an airplane. And, you know, you dance for the slow dances.

There were a lot of awkward silences between us; we didn't really talk. If you look at the picture, she looks miserable. I think maybe it's because it had been totally taken out of context; I knew her from somewhere, and we had a certain type of relationship, but we were now in a totally foreign environment.

And as a prom date, she was a disaster, because she looked ridiculous and she wasn't this sparkling person that was supposed to make me look good. On top of that, she wasn't fun. It was like she

had this plastic facade on, so it was like, Where is the cool chick? Once she put on the outfit, that was it; there was no sneaking out back for cigarettes or doing anything crazy.

So prom was like a nonevent, really. Once I realized we didn't win King and Queen of the Prom, I knew it really didn't matter. We left the prom and got into my parents' car. Luckily somebody had a gallon of vodka—just awful, cheap vodka—and we just started swilling it. Except she wouldn't drink, and at some point she was like, "I'm really tired and I want to go home," or "I have to do something tomorrow," or some excuse. I took her home and then I basically acted like the third wheel with my friend Greg and his date.

When I realized I wasn't gonna get laid, I damn well was going to get drunk. So I got very, very, very drunk. To the point that Greg made the

decision that I needed to be sobered up with coffee and he took me to his date's house at, like, three in the morning.

They sat me down. Somebody brought me coffee, which I slapped away and it landed on the ground and broke. Then the mother and father of Greg's date came downstairs and started yelling. The mother told the father to go back up and she told Greg to throw me in the cellar to sober up. They were going to throw me down the stairs to the cellar! Thank God, Greg said no. But I somehow fell over, and Greg stood on my chest so I couldn't get up. And I still remember the mother screaming, "Get him out of here. Get him out of here. Get him out of here."

Greg threw me in the car and drove me home. He crashed at my house that night, and I projectile-vomited all over my bedroom. The next morning he was so pissed at me, because he thought I had ruined his chances of getting laid. I don't think he was going to get laid, because he was a geek just like me, and neither of us were going to get laid. But I remember coming into school and hearing about who got laid and who was doing coke at the prom. And I was like, Coke, Jesus, I had enough trouble getting my jug vodka.

In retrospect, I think I was looking for a *Pretty in Pink* kind of a prom. And that really didn't happen. God, it was such a disappointment on so many levels. The pictures didn't even turn out good. So it wasn't like I had a disastrous prom and I could show people good pictures of it; it was disastrous *and* the photos were bad. I should put one on my mantel just for camp value, because it's so not me anymore. I can't throw them out, because they're prom pictures; it's almost like a sacred thing. A sacred thing I bombed at.

I never saw my date again. No, that's not true. After I got the pictures, I ran into her and asked her if she wanted them. I don't know if I gave them to her or not, but after that I didn't run into her at the train station anymore.

It's funny, I really don't think there's anyone I would have rather gone with. It wasn't about a person—it was about the perfect person. So I don't know if there was anyone . . . maybe Sandra Bernhard, but that's about it.

POSTSCRIPT

"Prom was like the rest of high school," says Steffan. "To me, it was all an unfortunate blur. And I always knew that better things lay ahead."

He was right: after high school, Steffan attended Clark University, came out, and moved to San Francisco, where he is now a successful graphic designer.

"It's funny, because it fades away and you don't even think about it until somebody comes along and drags it back up," jokes Steffan.

Steffan, a good sport, was kind enough to supply some sassy illustrations to the "Queer Themes" article in the Mini Mag that starts on page 77.

THE
DRAMA
QUEEN

REID DAVIS

Reid's father was in the Air Force, so he grew up all over the map. He was born in Fort Worth, Texas, but spent time in Little Rock, Arkansas, and then Guam. When Reid was in third grade, his family settled in Columbia, South Carolina.

But Reid fantasized about living in New York City. "I was growing up in South Carolina in sort of a state of disbelief," he says. "There was barbeque and there were rednecks, and I was just watching the clock, and watching a lot of Woody Allen movies thinking, When is my real life going to begin? Because this just can't be happening."

"Columbia never felt like home," adds Reid. "But the theater always did."

I WAS PROBABLY IN THE FOURTH GRADE when I did my first community theater play. I had been doing plays with kids in the neighborhood. We acted out all kinds of movies in the backyard, like *The Ten Commandments*. When I was in the third grade, we had this sketch comedy group and we entertained our fellow students at lunch. I created this sort of Julia Child-type character; I did this skit in drag where she was creating this lunch and everything fell apart. I ended up performing it for the whole school; that was probably my first real performance

> "One of the first plays I did was *Winnie the Pooh* and I played Piglet. That's where I met my first queen. His name was Randall."

thing. Then I heard there were auditions for the community theater and I knew I wanted to do that.

One of the first plays I did was *Winnie the Pooh* and I played Piglet. That's where I met my first queen. His name was Randall and he was the costume and makeup person. He was tall and thin; he had a very sunny disposition and he was effeminate, which both excited me and totally terrified me. I think he probably scared me because he scared my parents; they pretty much said, "You need to be careful of that guy." I don't remember if they said he's gay, but I figured it out. I mean, this was '74, and after the Stonewall riots, the *CBS Reports* documentary about "the Homosexuals" and all of the press; it was out there in the public arena.

The review of the play was "Blah, blah ... *Winnie the Pooh* ... entertaining family fare ... And, as Piglet, Reid Davis proves to be a promising young *actress*." It was a definite moment. It was horrifying to me, and totally embarrassing to my parents, but it was okay because I loved doing the show. It was this very exotic world of adulthood and I could be anything in that world. And these were my people.

I remember having a crush on a guy named Sammy who played Winnie the Pooh. He was a big, furry, teddy bear kind of guy. And this woman Ellen, who played the young mother of Christopher Robin, was vying for Miss South Carolina at the time—she had already won Miss Columbia. I think Sammy and Ellen totally knew I was gay and that I was dealing with being in Columbia, South Carolina, and they wanted to take me under their wing. At the end of the production there was this big trip to Hilton Head to go cheer on Ellen in her quest for Miss South Carolina. They wanted me to come along with them. Of course my parents didn't let me go, because I was like, "It's going to be so fun! We're gonna all stay in the same hotel room together, we're gonna jump up and down and scream for her!"

Growing up in an environment that was pretty homophobic, I guess the theater was sort of a refuge. But I started doing less theater in junior high. I don't think it's as simple as "the theater is the gay place" and that's why I stopped, but I do think that is a big part of it. The theater people were sort of on the fringe, they were not mainstream, and at the time it was really important to me to fit in.

I still did some theater, but I started getting more into academics and this Jewish youth group. And I started having crushes on boys. I had crushes on women too, but in retrospect, they were all a fantasy tied to the theater. I thought, If I can create a character, I can actually reinvent myself as straight if I want to. And it is seductive to a fifteen, sixteen-year-old gay boy to be straight.

But at the beginning of high school, I started to have sex with my friend Tim. He and I wrote comedy sketches together. And he was a soccer player . . . adorable. We had these elaborate rituals of how to get each other's clothes off. We had strip card games and we had, you know, I'm gonna play a song and if you can name the title, you have to take your shirt off. We would read about gay sex in *Everything You Always Wanted to Know About Sex*, and we would just experiment and experiment.

One night, Tim was like, "You know what I read about those guys"—it was

ABOVE AND RIGHT A YOUNG REID PLAYS PIGLET IN *WINNIE THE POO* **PREVIOUS PAGES** SNAPSHOTS FROM PROM NIGHT

always *those* guys—"they cornhole." And I was like, "Do you mean butt-fuck? We can try that, but do we have to call it cornhole?" So we tried, but we didn't really have any concept of lube or anything. So I can remember me really, really, really trying really, really hard to get my dick in him, and it just wasn't going anywhere.

When it came time for junior prom, I didn't have a date, because, well, I was in love with Tim. Even at the time, I knew prom was a performance, a show. And I knew who I really cared about. So I thought, Tim and I are each going to have a date, but we're really going to be there together.

I ended up asking this girl that I met through the Jewish youth group. I can't even remember her name. Let's call her Kim. She was this gorgeous, sweet, elegant girl from Charleston, which was ninety miles away—just far enough away for me to adore her and idolize her, but not close enough that I actually had to deal with it.

At the time, I was obsessed with the movie *Tess*. And I had several phone conversations with Kim and I was like, "Okay, all these Columbia girls are going to show up in lime-green taffeta dresses, it's all going to be fake, fake, fake." And I was like, "Have you seen *Tess*? Because in this movie Nastassja Kinski is wearing very simple, natural

fabrics and that's real beauty. And you have this real beauty." I probably also mentioned Barbra Streisand's wedding outfit in *A Star is Born*, because I was also fascinated with that. And Barbra wore those little white flowers in her hair—what are they called? Baby's breath. So I said, "If there's baby's breath, that would be okay, too."

I can still remember these conversations and going, "It's your dress, but this is what I think is really, really pretty." I mean, I didn't send her costume swatches or anything, which I probably would do now. So I did give her . . . you know, there was some room for her.

The whole arrangement was that I was going to go to Charleston and drive her back to Columbia. And I was like staging it: there was going to be like a surprise event; she really was going to come down the stairs like I was seeing her for the first time.

So I picked her up and she was beautiful. The dress was very close to my vision; it was like a pale yellow with rosy and green flowers and a nice, high waist. I thought she looked really, really beautiful. Her hair looked gorgeous, but no baby's breath. And I was probably thinking, Okay, how datey is this going to be?

Really, I was more excited about getting to the prom and being there with my friends and Tim. And I'm sure that if part of me was wanting to stage it, you know, for people to see me with this beautiful girl from another town, then another part of me was working on staging it so that we'd all be *so* tipsy that Tim and I could hang out and end the night together.

We had dinner at this fancy version of TGI Friday's. There was a small group of us. Charlie, who was my closest friend, was in love with a girl, Shelley, who was dating this other guy who Charlie didn't like. And I don't even remember who Tim was dating, but as far as I was concerned, the whole thing was really a date with me presented as something else.

By the time we got to the prom we were already pretty tipsy—we had stashed away magnums of something. The prom's theme was "A Night in Paris," and they had cardboard cut-outs of the Paris skyline and plastic champagne glasses. I knew that this was all the prom team could do, but I also knew that we could have really been transported through theatrical magic.

We danced. And I remember there was one song where the boys and the girls were dancing in two separate groups—it was like a Kool and

> # Even at the time, I knew prom was a performance. And I knew who I really cared about.

TOP REID DIRECTED THE WASHER WENCHES COMEDY TROUPE IN 1992 **ABOVE** REID AND HIS BOYFRIEND **RIGHT** WITH THE OTHER LOVE OF HIS LIFE, DANTE

the Gang song, probably "Celebration"—and the whole time I was thinking about Tim and that we were getting away with dancing together.

It was a fun evening. In a way, it was the perfect prom for a gay boy in Columbia, South Carolina—lots of romantic fantasies, a lot of acting things out, and a great undercurrent of real desire. Besides, there really weren't that many options. And it wasn't *Carrie*, you know.

I ended up having the after-party at my house. Kim was staying over, in a different bedroom; my parents were very clear about that. And I definitely wanted to avoid any kind of real contact with her, any funny business. And that seemed fine with her, too.

Tim didn't stay over; he probably went back to his house. At that point, Tim and I had already started to talk about where we were going to go after we graduated. And I remember really wanting to be more clear with him and say, "You know what? We've been sleeping together for two years, we spend all of our time together, we're actually dating." But he would sort of change the subject.

When I finally did say, "You know, I think I feel something, I think this is more," that's when it ended. We never had sex again.

As his relationship with Tim was cooling, Reid started sleeping with boys from a nearby college. "And I knew that it was happening: that I was going to have sex with men for the rest of my life."

Revisiting prom, he admits a few regrets: "I wanted to be on the prom committee, I wanted to really be in Paris, and I wanted to really be dating and dancing with Tim. Had it been possible then, it probably would have been less romantic in that it would have been more real. But Tim and I would have kissed in the end. And I would have loved that, just to show everyone."

Reid is still staging realities. He moved behind the curtain in college and launched a successful directing career. Along the way, Reid, who recently earned his PhD in Performance Studies and Film from Berkeley, has worked with teens and had the chance to employ lessons learned during his Piglet days. "The best scenario," he believes, "is for them to see examples of older people who are gay and who are proud and who can be there to talk to."

Tim, on the other hand, got married, became a filmmaker and let bygones be bygones. "Ten years after high school, we ran into each other and he was like, 'You know Reid, I tell everybody that you're my gay friend.' And I'm like, 'Hello, cornhole.'"

ELLYN - 1980

THE NEXT
BEST THING

MARIA - 1981

DIA

MICHAEL CALLAHAN

NORTHEAST HIGH SCHOOL
PHILADELPHIA, PENNSYLVANIA
CLASS OF **1981**

"There was a huge stigma attached to it. I grew up in a family where gays and blacks and Jews were just . . . you know, there were terrible things said," explains Michael, the youngest of four boys, who was raised in a conservative Irish-Catholic enclave of Northeast Philadelphia.

The slurs abated over time. "You know, people mellow out. But as I was growing up, being able to live as a gay person just seemed incomprehensible to me," adds Michael, now a successful writer and editor in Manhattan's homo-friendly world of magazine publishing. "People were expected to grow up, get married and buy the house two doors down from their parents."

Michael did his best to fit in. In high school, he explains, there were "the jocks and the girls who all looked like Farrah Fawcett. Then it slowly delineated from there. I aimed for the middle. You don't want to be the one whose school bag is getting kicked down the street, and you understand that you are not going to be the one on the homecoming court. I was reasonably successful: I never got beat up. And I was obviously a popular prom date."

I REMEMBER I WAS IN A POWDER-BLUE SUIT, and Ellyn, who was a big girl with a pretty face, was in a powder-blue dress. The dance floor was really packed; it was one of those "Stairway to Heaven" songs. And I remember looking around at everybody making out and thinking, This is what she wants. She expects this. I didn't really want to do it, but I just thought I should. And then I turned to her and kissed her. And I can remember feeling good about it, because my hetero credentials were on display. It was proof that I belonged there. Like, "See, I have a prom date and I'm making out with her and I'm doing all the things you're doing." It was like having my passport stamped.

> "I was completely central casting . . . I was chatty, I was nice and I was a good dresser. Those are things that sort of help when prom season comes around."

That was my first prom. I ended up getting my passport stamped six times: I went to my junior and my senior, I went to Maria Menetti's junior and senior, I went to Suzette Di Leone's junior and Diane Shattaquay's senior.

I was completely central casting. If you didn't have the love of your life or the dreamboat to go  with, I was absolutely the next best thing. Because I was funny, I was chatty, I was nice and I was a good dresser. Those are things that sort of help when prom season comes around; you know, it's all marketing.

And there was not one mother that didn't want her daughter to marry me. Forget about the prom; I heard back from them later that their mothers were like, "You need to date him," and "Why can't you date more guys like him?" Because I would come in and I could talk about anything. I could comment on their decor, but could also talk about the stock mar-

ket. If the dad was there and he was watching a baseball game, I certainly knew if the Phillies were in second place. I was courteous and got nice flowers. And I wasn't going to try anything—I definitely wasn't going to try anything.

I had done the prom thing— but I felt like if I didn't take her she wasn't gonna go.

That's why my friend Jamie asked me to take his sister Suzette to her prom. They were Filipino and if you know anything about Filipino culture, basically it's structured like this: Filipino guys are expected to go out with all the American girls they can and then marry a nice Filipino virgin, and Filipino girls are kept like Rupunzel until they marry a Filipino guy. Suzette was no exception. But she had a bunch of American girlfriends and she really wanted to go to her prom and I think she preyed upon her parents to let her.

The problem was they had to find a guy to go. So basically Jamie, I think, went, "Look, I work with this guy. I'll vouch for him. He'll fill the suit, he'll take a nice picture, and that'll be it." I was like the perfect Ken doll, literally with no penis. So her parents said, "Okay, that's fine." So Jamie came to me and asked, and I said okay. I liked Jamie—that's really what it was about. But that was a terrible prom. Suzette had no social skills because she had just never been around boys; she was just completely a deer in the headlights.

I never got the prom picture from her. Finally, I said to Jamie, "I want the picture. I paid, and I want the picture." Because I wanted proof. It took a while, but he finally got me a five-by-seven and a wallet.

I have no idea what happened to the five-by-seven, but years later my mother found all these random pictures lying around—including the wallet of me and Suzette—and made a collage of my prom dates. She glued these six pictures: three on the top and three on the bottom. It was like "The Best of Michael's Proms." She thought

LEFT WITH HIS BROTHERS IN 1977
RIGHT (IN PINK) VERY 1985 RIGHT DETAILS
FROM PROM COLLAGE MADE BY HIS MOTHER
PREVIOUS PAGES THE FULL COLLAGE; WITH
BROTHERS ON EASTER SUNDAY, 1965

that was hilarious. And it was funny to see my changing hairstyles and my changing fashion sense; I look worst in the first one and I look best in the last.

I was twenty-one when I went to that last one. My brother had gotten married. The bridesmaid I was paired up with at his wedding was this girl named Diane, who my sister-in-law had babysat for. Of course, she was a heavy girl. Cute, but the kind where you say, "Oh she has such a pretty face. It's such a shame." And so she was desperate to go to her senior prom and she discretely inquired to my sister-in-law, "Do you think Michael would take me if I asked him?" So my sister-in-law came to me and said, "Look, Diane wants to go, would you take her?"

I did *not* want to go—I had done the prom thing—but I felt like if I didn't take her she wasn't gonna go. I knew how important it was to go to your prom, so I did it. I got a fabulous tux: white dinner jacket and black pants and a black tie, which my father wore at his wedding and I had always admired. Unfortunately, she dressed in a gown that was like Scarlet O'Hara—it was literally a hoopskirt and I could barely fit it in my car. It was a little bit overdone . . . Actually, it was a lot overdone and I was pretty embarrassed.

I made out with her that night. I liked kissing girls; it was fun, you know, and it felt good. (Of course, at that point, I had nothing to compare it to.) She was very Cinderella about it; I mean, it was very important to her. And I had signed on to this, so I really needed to do it the way it should be done. To this day, I think if you asked her, she would say, "Oh yeah, I had a wonderful time at my prom." I don't think she'd say, "I had the most amazing night of my life." But I think I delivered. You know, I came through.

I didn't try to go to so many proms, but I was willing. Now, I think it's absurd, but at the time it was a measure of my desirability as a heterosexual teen and I had such insecurity about my masculinity and about my attractiveness. Also, I was attracted to the glamour and the ritual of prom. It was something I identified with really early; when I was eight, my brother went to his prom and I can remember all the hoopla, and I thought it was amazing that you could be a teenager and get to play dress-up.

Still, you know, I was a really late bloomer in the gay game. I can't tell you how many friends have stories where they're like, "Oh, I was

I sat in my living room and thought, Alright, if we try to undo all of this, could we do it? Could I survive it?

twelve-years-old, and Jimmy down the street and I were playing find-the-pencil." When I was twelve-years-old, I was watching *Superfriends* and eating HoHos.

I didn't come out 'til I was thirty. I had a mad crush on a guy in college and we ended up becoming best friends. He was the first guy I was in love with—he was probably the great love of my life—but he got married. I was in his wedding.

I ended up sleeping with him after he got married. By then, I certainly knew what the deal was with my sexuality, but I was still trying to make it work. At one point, when I was twenty-six, I said, "Okay, if I construct my life the way my brothers have, I can do this." So I bought a house; I drove a car similar to the ones they did; I got a job similar to the ones they had; and I dated a girl who was similar. I just thought, If I get all of the pieces of the puzzle in place, then the pieces will fit.

My girlfriend Patricia and I even began to plan our wedding: We would get married in her church 'cause that was what was traditional. She wanted to have the reception at this place called the Rose Briar, which was where all the better Northeast Philadelphia brides had their weddings. We even got so far as to say, "How many people do we want to have?" and "Who would you invite?"

Planning the wedding, that part was fun. But the more we did it, the more panicky I got. Because, well it wasn't like prom. It wasn't this fancy thing that is just one night and you get to play Rhett Butler and then walk away from it. This was much more serious: a commitment for the rest of our lives, ostensibly.

Eventually I became so depressed about how fucked up I had made my life. Then one day I called in sick to work and I sat in my living room in my fabulous home and I thought, Alright, if we try to undo all of this, could we do it? Could I survive it? And I remember getting out a yellow legal pad and writing down everything I'd have to do to undo it—it was a long list. And I just thought, If you don't do it, you're gonna wrap your car around a tree someday. Because you cannot, you can't run from you.

That was the day I decided to start over. That was in November of 1992. I slowly and covertly put all these pieces in motion. And in April of 1993, I did it. I went to my parents after work—and I'll never forget it—they were sitting at the dining room table and they were just like, "So what's new?" And I just vomited it out. I said, "Okay here's the deal. I have some news: I'm leaving the gas company and I've taken a job with a small magazine up in Northern New Jersey and I'm selling the house and I'm breaking it off with Patricia and I'm moving in three weeks."

I didn't say I was gay. But my mother—mothers always know—she looked at me with this look, like she knew what it was. And she said to me, "I think you should do what you have to do." But she knew what it was really about. Even though we didn't say it out loud.

POSTSCRIPT

Michael came out to his family a year and a half later. "I spent that time eating myself into oblivion, because I was so stressed out. Then I figured out, Okay now that I'm coming out, I have to lose all this weight in order to be marketable. It was like reliving high school again."

While he tries not focus on it, Michael battles with what-could-have-been. "When I was eighteen I had a really good body. I had fabulous hair and good skin and I had a nice chest and a great ass . . . and I was sleeping with no one! I was home watching the *Love Boat*."

While he regrets spending his youth in the closet and not on Christopher Street, he realizes that it may have been for the best. "It's so interesting: there are paths that you think you want to take but, in fact, you probably don't. I was so impressionable back then; I could have ended up in porno or a crackhead."

He's also aware that he could have ended up dead. "My prom was in 1981 . . . the year before AIDS hit. If I had come out then, guns blazing so to speak, I might not be around today. I mean, that generation got wiped out."

That is why Michael says he tends to date younger men. "My generation just doesn't exist. They either got married—just panicked and settled down—or they died. You can't find a guy who's forty-two. You just can't . . . they're not around."

MISS POPULARITY

ANA OTIS

DWIGHT MORROW HIGH SCHOOL
ENGLEWOOD, NEW JERSEY
CLASS OF **1980**

How popular was Ana in high school? "I made up a fake club just to see. It was called the Space Cadets and everyone wanted to join it," says the forty-one-year-old vice president of her family's music publishing company. "Back then it was popular to get T-shirts made with names on it and stuff. Well, I had a T-shirt that said 'Space Cadet.' Next thing you know, everybody had T-shirts that said, 'Space Cadet.'"

Even after Sapphic rumors spread through the hallways, Ana remained atop the high-school food-chain. "I was a nice person. You know, it wasn't like I was a bitch on wheels," she explains.

"To tell you the truth, I think being with women added to my notoriety. People were like, 'That girl's just crazy, she'll do anything.'"

"At that time I didn't know that shame was supposed to be prescribed to this type of thing. I never really heard anybody saying anything bad about it," says Ana, whose tight-knit family lived in a liberal, tony suburb alongside a lot of other entertainment folk, including music legend Dizzy Gillespie who, as a child, Ana affectionately called "Uncle Dizzy."

I HAD A DIFFERENT TYPE OF SCHOOL situation, because when I was about seven I started singing professionally. I was a backup singer in the original cast of *Sesame Street* and I also did *Electric Company* and all this voice-over stuff.

I went to all public schools all the way through to Dwight Morrow High. And high school was a blast. I was extremely popular: I was voted class clown, I was a captain of the steel drum band and I was the lead in the senior play, *Guys and Dolls*. I mean, I was *really* popular. It was weird. As a matter of fact, Sister Souljah—she was Lisa Williamson back then—used to warn this guy not to hang out with me; she told him I had a cult. And it really was almost like a cult!

My group of friends, let's see, what do I have to say about my friends? Well, I had this one friend named Michelle that I used to really, really love. And I used to hang out with her a lot; we were in steel drums together and stuff. She was straight, and as time went along I started realizing that I was more and more gay and started acting on it. Once she confronted me and asked if I was gay, because she had heard some rumors. And I didn't deny it, you know; I confirmed it. And that was the last she spoke to me. We had been best friends for years. That sucked, man. Majorly. I still think about her every now and then.

But I had a lot of friends to take up the slack. And I started hanging around with a different crowd of these kids that

> ## "High school was a blast. I was voted class clown, I was a captain of the steel drum band and I was the lead in the senior play."

were really artistic and really talented. Like Regina Belle and Cindy Miesel—she sings background for Luther Vandross. We would show up at a dance and start dancing, and then the whole place would like form a circle around us. We would make up our own dances and people would try and learn them.

One guy in our crowd was Cubie Burke. I started going out with him, but we were both bi. You know, we were doing our own

> # I was rubbing Tracy's back. Next thing you know, my hands are up her shirt and we are throwing down!

thing. To me, our arrangement was that I wouldn't sleep with any other men and he wouldn't sleep with any other women. I mean, we'd go on a double date and switch; it was weird, man, really experimental.

In hindsight, I realized that I always liked girls. I always had crushes on my female teachers or on the effeminate male teachers. I always was particularly close to one little girlfriend or another.

The sexual aspect didn't surface until this young girl, like a fourteen-year-old freshman, kissed me when I was—I had to be probably seventeen because I was driving—so it was senior year. Her name was also Lisa. Now she plays professional women's football. So, we were rehearsing for *Guys and Dolls* and we were spending a lot of time together. One day, Lisa tells me that she wants to take me out to lunch. So we go to some fast-food joint, and she started telling me about how she's been with this twenty-eight-year-old woman. Then she's like, "But really I'm in love with this girl and she doesn't even know I'm alive." And she starts asking me all of this advice on how to get this girl, and so I'm telling her all that I know—my being a whole three years older than her.

So I'm dropping her off and we're sitting in her driveway and she turns to me and says, "You know the girl I was telling you about? It's you." And she leans in and kisses me on the mouth and jumps

out of the car and runs away. So that took me for a loop, but immediately I was mega-curious. So I was like, Okay, huh, I want to see where this is going. Well, it went into a strange, obsessive, weird thing; Lisa really had a big crush on me, but I didn't really like her that much. I mean, I liked her, but I wasn't really like into her. And she kissed like an iguana, and I was like, Oh my God, I can't get with it.

Now, we had a mutual friend named Tracy. And Tracy and I started talking on the phone a lot and stuff. And Tracy started telling me that she has feelings for girls. The next time we were together, we were at this girl's house having this party. Lisa was there, too. And man, I was rubbing Tracy's back and feeling mad electricity—I mean currents. And I pretended to be upset and I went upstairs where everybody wasn't. And of course she came up later to check on me. And next thing you know, my hands are up her shirt and we are throwing down!

She was like seriously my first love; she used to run up to my house from miles away to come and see me. But she was torture, because she was one of those girls that didn't want to be gay, but just kept kissing. People would see us and then she'd be pissed off with me and she didn't want to talk to me for a while. I guess that I started to feel, Oh maybe there's something that's not right because she's freaking out like this. But I really didn't, I just never felt any guilt about it.

By the time prom came, Cubie and I had broken up; besides, Cubie is two years younger, so I wasn't about to go with a sophomore. I probably could have gotten away with taking Tracy—people would have thought it was just another one of my crazy stunts—but it didn't even occur to me. Plus, Tracy was freaked out about people finding out about us.

But I had an arrangement with this guy Patrick, who was like the most popular guy in school. He was really, really good looking and a star on the track team; any girl would've loved to have gone to the prom with him. Years before, he and I had said that we were going to go to the prom together. At this time, he had left our school, but since I didn't have a date, I called on my deal with him.

A IZA,
these few wo...
would like to say
you; I want you to enjoy
w that you are !! I
PERSON !! I
TOGETHER the few little
pending are one of my
You are one of Persons
Enjoyed
ANA, you make y
because yo
sum. I have not k
as the like to
PERSON. I Alrig fore
ould have and you

I was very upset actually, because he was late. At first I thought he wasn't even going to show up.

I don't really think Pat wanted to take me to the prom, since he didn't go to the school anymore. And we weren't romantic with each other or anything like that; I had a big crush on him for a while, but we were never romantic.

Now, the prom was a big deal in Englewood. Of course there was a lot of buildup. It was going to be like the best night. We were going to party, party, party. And that was like the first night that you could stay out of the house all night long into the morning with your parents' permission and their car. You were gonna go and just be beautiful and you were going to have the greatest time with your guys. And you had to make sure that you were going with the right person and wearing the right dress, and that your date was wearing the right tux and stuff.

I always imagined that the guy would wear a tux to match my gown. You know, I wasn't really a gown person—I'm more like a corduroy and chino type of girl—but I wore a pale-yellow gown. And my mom actually got me the dress and then she changed it up to make it a little more to my liking. I'm sort of androgynous, I guess; I can feel butch sometimes and I can feel femmy too. And prom was definitely a femmy evening.

I was a little upset when Pat picked me up. I was very upset actually, because he was late. At first I thought he wasn't even going to show up, and that was really painful. He was late because he had a problem with his tux. Initially he didn't want to wear a tux—he's not a tux kind of guy—but then he got the tux and the pants didn't fit. So he ended up wearing a double-breasted suit. He looked good, but I was still mad, because I felt like, Oh, now he's not going to look proper.

Anyway, my father lent Pat his new Town Car, so we drove over to the place and everything was really beautiful. And of course my mood lightened: we were having a good time; all my friends were there and everybody looked really great; and we had a great table. Also, Pat was a good dancer. So we got out on the floor and we were getting down. Oh man, it was really good music back then. Like Parliament-Funkadelic and Evelyn Champagne King. Sugar Hill Gang had just come out and rap had just started. So, you know, I ended up having a good time at the prom.

Afterwards, I wanted to go to some disco in New York. And Pat was like, "Well, you know, I don't really want to drive your father's car too much." And I'm like, "Why didn't you say that before? We could have gotten a limo or been in a limo with some other people and then we wouldn't have to worry about it." But he wanted to drive the new car. I was really kind of pissed, you know? So I was like, "Come on, we *are* going to this disco." And we all went to New York City and met at this club Xenon. After that some people were going to hotels, getting in with the hanky panky stuff, you know.

I think we might have just stayed at the club for a while and then gone home. So I ended up coming home too early and not having as much fun as I would liked to have had.

POSTSCRIPT

Ana hasn't seen or talked to Patrick in more than twenty years. "I talk to his sister and she fills me in on what's going on with him."

She's still best friends with Tracy, who became more comfortable with her homosexuality. "We messed around for years after that, my God, I mean like ten, twelve years," says Ana. "We would have girlfriends and we'd still mess around every now and then."

Unfortunately, Ana's parents, who had gay friends when Ana was a kid, were less than accepting when their daughter came out to them three years after prom. "My mom didn't speak to me for six months and she was praying every day."

For a long time Ana couldn't bring lovers to the house or family occasions. Afraid she might be outed in the press, she also kept her life low key and under wraps, which, as you might imagine, is not really her style.

"After years of being the little black sheep, I finally told them, 'Listen, I'm holding my life back. And I'm doing it because I don't want to embarrass you guys, but I want to live my life. I need to do my thing.'"

While her parents seem to be coming around—Ana can now bring girlfriends to the house—she still believes, "it's a matter of everybody just losing their shame."

MOST
UNLIKELY
TO SUCCEED

DAN STEWART

CUMBERLAND HIGH SCHOOL
CUMBERLAND, RHODE ISLAND
CLASS OF **1980**

"The simple, obvious thing would have been to go to the senior prom with a girl. But that would have been a lie—a lie to myself, to the girl, and to all the other students," wrote Aaron Fricke in his memoir *Reflections of a Rock Lobster*, which chronicled his personal and legal struggle to attend his senior prom with another male, Paul Guilbert.

Classmate Dan Stewart, who would become the first openly gay person elected mayor in New York State, was involved in the groundbreaking court case that made it illegal to deny same-sex couples entry to the prom in the United States.

But his role is not what you'd think: Dan was one of the most outspoken objectors on television and radio during Aaron's clash with the school.

"I just wanted to lash out because I didn't want to be gay," explains Dan. "I thought that lashing out would be a better way of me not ever being considered to be a gay person. It was a case of, Doth thou protest too much?"

I T WAS A TYPICAL HIGH SCHOOL: you had your athletic types, you had your pot-smoking types, you had your brains, you had your nerds, you had everything. It wasn't a very diverse school; it was mostly white, some Portuguese, but that's about it.

I was a druggie, so I fit in pretty good. I was pretty popular; I could travel in any circle. It didn't matter what it was, I could fit in. But then again, I was scared to death of who and what I was.

> "I went to the library and looked up 'homosexuality' in the index-card file. And I read about how it was a sickness."

When I was very young, around ten-years-old or so, I started to think, Oh man, something different's going on here, and I didn't understand what it was. Of course, in my early teen years, well I don't know if it's experimenting or what the hell you call it, but there was definitely activity with other boys. And I was never attracted to girls, anyway.

I remember, probably my freshman or sophomore year, I went to the library in Cumberland and looked up "homosexuality" in the index-card file, scared to death that someone was watching me. I found a book on homosexuality and then pulled out another book on whatever it was—something non-controversial—and took the homosexual book and put it inside that one so I could read a few pages. And I read about how it was a sickness and

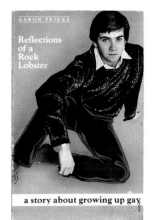

AARON FRICKE
Reflections of a Rock Lobster

a story about growing up gay

an illness. This was written in the '70s, before the whole medical community had come around and said, No, it's not like that. So there was some real nasty stuff in there. And that's what I thought I was; I thought, Oh my God, I'm one of these perverts.

Junior year, Paul Guilbert tried to take a guy to the prom and it was the talk on the CB radio. In the '70s, CBs—Citizen Band radios—were big. I

remember being on there all the time and people were all outraged this was happening and how bad it was for Cumberland. We went through that for a year, and Paul was turned down by the school's principal, Mr. Lynch. And that was the end of it.

Then, my senior year, all of a sudden talk started coming about Aaron's wanting to go to the prom with a guy. And it immediately became the talk of the town again. I, of course, was back on the CB, and then I was on TV, and then I was on AM radio—doing everything I could to speak out against these guys.

I think my fear of being gay came out in me responding the way I did. I didn't really know Paul or Aaron, and I had nothing against these guys. If anything, deep down inside, I supported 'em, but outwardly I couldn't do it.

The news stations started coming out to the high school and they started interviewing students. And that was the first time I ever ended up in an interview. And they were asking, "Well, what do you think?" And I said, "This is terrible because I'm going to the military and everybody's going to know that I'm from Cumberland and that's where the gay guys go to proms together . . . and they're dirty and they're just ruining our prom." And that's how I started to lash out, and then I couldn't get enough of it.

When I saw myself on TV, I felt really cool. I felt as though I was sticking up for how the local majority felt. I was speaking for everybody. Look, I was a dumb kid, but I was speaking what my parents thought; I was speaking what my friends' parents were thinking. Of course, people were like, "Oh hey way to go . . . Saw you on TV—you did great! . . . Will you stop these guys from doing this?"

And it's strange how my curiosity on the whole thing developed. It became a major court case, and I actually skipped school to go to the court room. The decision was going to be coming down and, for some reason, I *had* to be there. It didn't mean hide nor hair that I was there, but inside I was so interested in what was going to happen. Maybe it was a glimmer of hope: that these guys would be able to go.

Well, I went to the prom with this girl Jeanie; she was my *supposed* girlfriend. She was my best friend's sister. And we hung out a lot and people thought that when we left high school, we'd probably

I think my fear of being gay came out in me responding the way I did.

get married. Inside I knew that could never happen, especially with me riding off to the military. But it was a natural thing that I would ask her to go. So, we went.

We met at a friend's house, where we started out our prom night. You know, we had gotten dressed up, we got our tuxes and the flowers and all that stuff. In fact, the TV news had called me and asked for an interview before going to the prom, and so I did. Then it was just off to the prom.

And the media blitz was insane. So I don't know that any of us will ever remember that prom as being a normal prom, because it wasn't. And because of all the attention, I think it really took away from what a prom is supposed to be, which is a great, fun time for people who are together, to go and have fun. And it wasn't like that, because of all the attention and tension. Probably a lot of people didn't go because of it.

In the end, I actually did something that supported Aaron and Paul. When I arrived, one of the local TV stations interviewed me and the people going into the prom. And they gave me a camera with two minutes of tape on it. And they said, "They won't allow cameras in from the stations. But can you get us two minutes of film, get it out of the prom, give it to us, and we'll have an exclusive to run it?" I said, "Sure."

So I took the camera and I walked into the prom with it and people are looking at me, especially the media people like, "What the hell

Court clears way for male couple to go to prom tonight

By KAREN ELLSWORTH
Journal-Bulletin Staff Writer

The U.S. Court of Appeals in Boston refused yesterday to stay Judge Raymond J. Pettine's decision allowing a homosexual Cumberland High School senior to take a male escort to the senior prom tonight.

V. James Santaniello, the Cumberland

day in U.S. District Court in Providence, Judge Pettine ruled that Fricke has a constitutional right to attend the prom with another male as a political statement about human rights.

★ ★ ★

CUMBERLAND school officials had denied Fricke permission to go to the dance with a male escort because they

intend
decisi

FIR
Coffin
and H
the-de
ment
The r

Alt
the a
tine's

Plattsburgh's new mayor

Daniel Stewart traveled far on lessons of honesty and forgiveness

By MICHAEL CORKERY
Special to the Journal

PLATTSBURG, N.Y. — Daniel Stewart made his political debut on the steps of U.S. District Court in Providence.

It was the spring of 1980. A classmate at Cumberland High School, Aaron Fricke, was petitioning Chief Judge Raymond J. Pettine for the right to take a male date to the senior prom.

Stewart, looking outraged, railed against homosexuality for the television cameras camped outside the courthouse.

This month, Stewart, 37, made a different sort of debut. Stewart became the mayor of Plattsburgh, N.Y., an industrial city on the western shores of Lake Champlain.

And he's the first openly gay mayor of a city in New York State.

"I'm an example of how you can go from one point in your life to another," Stewart said. "Years ago, you could have told me I wouldn't amount to

anything, but I have."

In November, he defeated Democratic incumbent Clyde Rabideau, a fixture in Plattsburgh politics for more than a decade.

The vote was close: Stewart, a Republican city councilor, won by only 100 votes out of more than 5,500 cast. He defeated Rabideau on his own turf,

OPPORTUNITIES: Nicole Grube, and Stewart attend

winning the support of the police union and capturing five of the city's six wards.

STEWART HAS SUCCEEDED in the most unlikely of places.

Plattsburgh voters 20 years ago elected a Roman Catholic priest as their mayor. This time they chose a used-car salesman who candidly talks about his past drug and alcohol problems.

Stewart's victory shocked even some of his supporters.

"When people woke up the next morning, they were still pinching themselves to see if it really happened," said Chris Ortloff, a state legislator and chairman of the Clinton County Republicans. "There was a whole lot of things that you think would not get him elected."

In an era of presidents who smoke marijuana but don't inhale, of presidential candidates who used drugs but won't say what kind, Stewart is a different breed of politician.

he's got that thing for?" And I remember walking into the place and I saw the vice-principal and the principal, Mr. Lynch. And I went up and I said, "Mr. Lynch, channel twelve gave me this. They want me to take film of Aaron and Paul, and I don't want to do this." And he said, "Okay, come on." And we both walked out with the camera into the parking lot and gave it back to the people from the station. He gave some choice words to them, and then we went back in. And I remember, later in the evening, when Paul and Aaron started dancing together, I clapped with everybody else in the room. Which was weird.

They really were pioneers. That was one of the most courageous things that ever happened in the gay culture. It's just like out in San Francisco with Harvey Milk, you know, same story. Stonewall riots, same thing. It was something that probably raised the spirits and the hopes of every gay person in the country that knew about it.

Seventeen years later, I got a phone call from an organizer of the Gay Pride in Providence asking me if I was the same Dan Stewart from Cumberland, Rhode Island, who was now an openly gay city councilor in Plattsburgh, New York. He said, "Maybe since you're the same guy, you'd want to come down and maybe talk to us." So I went down, and there were a few thousand people. And I got up to give a speech and I had tears coming down my face. And I apologized; I made a public apology for what I had done seventeen years earlier.

Being an individual who is a recovering drug addict and alcoholic, and dealing with those issues, it's very important to be honest and try to make amends wherever possible for people I've hurt. And I felt as though I'd done a grave injustice to the gay community in Rhode Island. Going down there and doing that was definitely a way to get the monkey off my back. Because that was one of the pieces of shame left in my life that I hadn't taken care of. I felt much better about myself as a human being after that.

Paul emailed me, I think it was after I was elected mayor, so it was probably sometime in 2000. He said he didn't even remember much of the stuff that was going on, and that he had read about the speech and said there were "no hard feelings."

I tried to contact Aaron and never tracked him down. And I wanted to make amends with him, I wanted to say, "Hey look, maybe I didn't play an important part in your life, but you certainly played one in mine"; what I did was self-devastating and caused me anguish for years and years. And maybe I deserved that. And maybe if society was better, none of us would do that type of thing.

My prom, I guess, for the most part really sucked, because I didn't have the opportunity to be who I was. And that's the sad part of it. But I did not have an idol; I did not have someone to look up to who said "I'm gay." All I saw was the Bee Gees. I had sports heroes, but the most important person I could probably ever have related with at that age would have been another gay person. And I had no one to go to. Today, kids have people to go to, because there's so many open people.

LEFT TOP THE MAYOR TAKES PART IN A PLATTSBURGH PARADE
BOTTOM ARTICLE IN PROVIDENCE PAPER ABOUT A HOMETOWN BOY WHO MADE GOOD

POSTSCRIPT

It's all come full circle: Dan, out and serving as mayor of Plattsburgh, New York, is now a role model for queer teens. He even mentored a friend's cousin, who was contemplating suicide. With Dan's support, the teen came out to his parents and classmates, and was elected the first openly gay class president at Plattsburgh High.

"He went to the prom with his boyfriend," notes Dan. "I was so proud of him for that, because that's something I tried to stop before. It was a total turn of events from 1980."

Dan's journey was a little longer and a lot more complicated than his friend's cousin. After graduation, he enlisted in the Air Force, hoping to cure his gayness. "It's the God's honest truth: I thought I would become straight in the military." After serving for eight years, during which he too contemplated suicide, Dan drove tractor trailers, was homeless for a bit, came out to family and friends, and got into politics.

As opposed to being a liability, this rare queer Republican believes that "being gay in politics has opened more doors for me than my colleagues who are heterosexual." During the 2000 election, for example, he was called to Austin to give George W "some Gay 101."

But he has struggled to prove he's more than "an openly gay mayor" to a media intent on attaching his sexuality to every action and issue. "It got to the point where we had openly gay potholes," says Dan, who was re-elected in 2001.

THE
PROM
QUEEN

LOIS KASTEN

RIO RANCHO HIGH SCHOOL
ALBUQUERQUE, NEW MEXICO
CLASS OF **1980**

Lois Kasten

"My parents adored him," says Lois, the former Prom Queen about her prom date Patrick Mulhall. "They always thought that Pat and I were gonna get married."

Well, Patrick and Lois both turned out to be gay. And while they didn't wed, their friendship has lasted a quarter century, longer than most marriages. During that time, Patrick and Lois came out, found the loves of their lives, moved across the country and back to New Mexico, lost parents and tried to stay in touch.

What's the secret to their connection? "For both of us, nothing is sacred," explains Pat, who keeps their prom picture in a frame on his dresser. "Everything can be made fun of."

Adds Lois, "When I told Pat that I was gay, he started laughing, and he said, 'Ha ha! So am I!' It was, like, even a *better* friendship."

LOIS I MET PAT IN HIGH SCHOOL. Somewhere in high school, but I can't really remember the time. I have the old-lady memory. He's got a really great memory. But, let's say we met and we just clicked.

PAT IT WAS IN 1976. They had simultaneous pageants: Miss Rio Rancho and Miss Bicentennial. Lois was running, and I was helping out. A friend of mine was working with the pageant and said they needed someone to work backstage. Since I was in theater, I figured, Oh what the hell, it's worth a shot. It was really kinda dumb, but I got to meet Lois.

The two of us just cracked each other up, because we were making fun of everyone else in the pageant. Of course, when she came in first runner-up for Miss Bicentennial, her parents were ecstatic and she was mortified.

Lois is not what you'd call "drop dead gorgeous." And her parents got her into beauty pageants; I guess they thought she had low self-esteem—why they thought that I'll never know.

LOIS I loved high school. I just talked to everybody. I'd hang out with the dopers, because I'd walk through their area, and I'd hang out with the musicians and the drama people. I even knew the janitors. It didn't really matter to me what you did, you know? If you were cool with me, that was cool. I also did a lot of the extracurricular things: I was on the yearbook committee and I cheered. I was actually head cheerleader, if you can imagine.

I don't know if this makes a difference, but I was not out in high school, because I didn't know. I don't know if an out cheerleader would have had a shitty time in high school. Pat's told me some stories that he used to get the shit beat out of him, and it absolutely breaks my heart.

Lois Kasten

Lois, on the other hand, was one of the most popular girls in school. The sports guys loved to be around her, because she is just hilarious and can make anybody feel comfortable and at home. So I always thought she had hundreds of guys to date, and I thought it was kinda odd that she asked me to go to prom, but then I realized she never really had a steady boyfriend.

I'm two years older, so I was in college at the time and she called me and said: "Pat, you want to take me to my high school prom?" And I said "Sure, I'd love to." She didn't tell me until the night of the prom that she was running for Prom Queen. I, of course, thought it was hilarious.

LOIS Even though I was a cheerleader and this and that, I didn't have a lot of dates, you know, maybe because I wasn't going to put out. So, I would have had to ask somebody else to prom if it wasn't Pat, because nobody would have asked me.

But it was never an option that I wasn't gonna go to the prom. I helped put it together; I was involved with getting the place for prom, the decorations, the band, you know, just the whole glitter stuff that goes along with that. And I thought, I'm not busting my ass and not going to prom. So I asked Pat.

I always felt really comfortable with him. I could be open and I just didn't want to have stress about wondering whether someone was going to kiss me or make moves on me. And, as I mentioned, back then I didn't know that I was a lesbian; I was uncomfortable with men, but I didn't know why.

I never knew that, I would have *certainly* defended him. I would have been in people's faces, you know, "How can you do this to anyone, let alone my friend?" So, I think he had a different time than I did in high school. But I just . . . it seemed like I got along with everybody.

PAT I wasn't extremely popular. I was kind of a drama nerd. And being gay, it was tougher for me. I was always an easy target because I didn't know how to fight. One time, there was a group of eight girls that kicked the shit out of me. And they were like, "Patrick got beat up by girls!" And I thought, Well yeah, eight against one! But nobody saw the logic in it.

It wasn't every day, but it was kind of rough. And the funny thing is that I never thought that I was miserable; I just assumed that's the way it was: there were the groups that were picked on all the time and there were the groups that did the picking on.

ABOVE LOIS'S SENIOR PICTURE
RIGHT LOIS CHEERING IN COLLEGE
PREVIOUS PAGES LOIS AND PAT AT PROM; A YOUNG LOIS

Pat,

I have so much to say to you. You are like a brother to me. You helped me through my tears at abo... I miss you like hell. I'll see you this su... love you. ...remember you...

The night of the prom, I was kind of like a little schoolgirl—excited about Pat coming to get me. I don't think we stayed in my house real long. He probably just came in and said hi to my mom and dad, and then we hit the road.

When I got to the prom, I was kinda disappointed because some other girls had the same dress. But that was no big deal. The whole Prom Queen thing wasn't like, "Oh my God, I have to look glamorous, because I'm running for Prom Queen." I was more excited about being with Pat and just having a great time and seeing the whole thing come off.

When it was time to announce the Prom Queen, they had us all line up. We just kinda stood with our dates. Then they called my name and I was like, "Oh my God." It was pretty exciting.

Once I was crowned, the band asked me, "What would you like to hear?" And the only thing that came to my head was "Desperado." So they played "Desperado" for Pat and me to dance. And afterward people were congratulating me and hugging me.

I remember calling my dad and telling him that I was Prom Queen, and he was pretty excited. Then I had a little tiff with some witch who ran for Prom Queen too. I can't remember if we were in the bathroom or if we were on the railing of the stairs, but she came up to me and went off on me about how I'm this and that, and I'm not even pretty. And I was like, "Fuck you. First of all, you're wearin' some dead animal around your neck"—not cool—"and you know what? You can have the crown, I don't care. What's important is people thought enough about me to vote for me."

PATRICK MULHALL: DECA, 3-4; Flag Corp, 4; German Club, 2-3; Thespian & Drama Club, 2-4; Staters, 4.

At our twenty-year reunion, she came up to me and apologized. She said she was just absolutely mortified, thinking about it as an older person, that she actually had that confrontation with me. I was like, "Don't even worry about it, it's no biggie!" She was actually the highlight of the prom.

PAT The worst part was that this poor girl had no chance of winning, because she was just pathetic. She was wearing her mother's mink stole to the prom and what looked like a dress from the '60s. And I felt sorry for her, because it wasn't

I always thought she had hundreds of guys to date, so I thought it was kinda odd that she asked me.

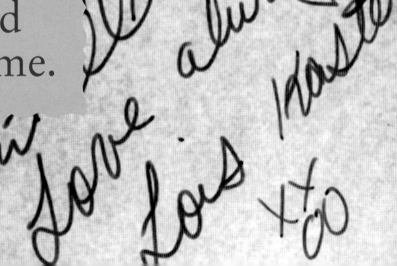

I remember calling my dad and telling him that I was Prom Queen, and he was pretty excited.

cool to dress in the '60s back then. It was just out of fashion.

Anyway, a bunch of us went out after the prom to the Village Inn Pancake House for breakfast, and sat around talking and having fun. Then I brought Lois home and I kissed her *on the cheek* good night . . . there was no tongue involved in this relationship.

LOIS I had no sexual anything until I was in college. My first kiss was with a woman and it was my sophomore year. I was in ROTC in college. You're gonna die when I tell you why: I wanted to run and sing songs with a group of people. Freshman year, every single morning at five-thirty a.m., ROTC ran by my dorm room, singing cadences. And I thought, Man, that would be cool. So I went to the ROTC office and signed up. And then I went to boot camp at Fort Knox, Kentucky; I met my first partner there.

We just started hanging out together and we went out one evening and we were sitting down, and I looked at her and told her, "I really like you." And she said, "Well, I like you too." And I said that I *really* liked her and that I'd like to kiss her. She was kinda freaked. She said, "I've never ever, ever been with a straight woman before, and you're going home to Albuquerque and I'm going home to North Carolina, and I'm not gonna wreck your life." And I said, "You know what? This is kinda my decision too." So, anyway that was my first kiss. And then I fell madly in love with her.

I was devastated when I had to say goodbye. And I got home to Albuquerque and it was very hard. I couldn't talk to my parents about it, because that was just taboo. My dad actually opened a letter of mine and confronted me about it. And I told him. I told him, "I'm in love with a woman, I met her at boot camp, and that's just the way it is." It was not a good scene.

You know, I was always my daddy's little girl. If he came to pick me up from cheerleading practice, I would kiss him hello; I would hold his hand. But he kicked me out of the house. He disowned me; he lit a candle for me as if I was dead. He took every single thing in my room and burned it. My clothes, my shoes, my crown, my letter jacket. He just, he destroyed my room and he didn't talk to me for ten years. I tried to be in touch with him, and I wrote to him, but

LEFT TOP PATRICK AT HIS SENIOR PROM LEFT BOTTOM LOIS IN
ROTC **ABOVE** PATRICK, LOIS, BART AND ANNE IN 2003
RIGHT PATRICK AND LOIS IN 2003

he just didn't respond. There was not a day that went by in ten years that I didn't think about him. But for the first time in my life, I chose my happiness over pleasing my parents. And it was really—it was a great thing, but it was hard.

PAT I spoke to Lois's mom very briefly about it. The Hadassah organization in Rio Rancho was having a latke fundraiser, and my mother and I went—I took my mother a lot of places. I ran into Mrs. Kasten there. She, of course, adored me and gave me a big hug and a kiss hello. And I said, "How is Lois?" And she said, "We don't speak of Lois; in our minds she's dead." It did surprise me, and I was like, "How can you do that?" And she said, "You don't understand: in the Jewish religion, she has brought shame upon our family."

It was intense, especially since I had no way of getting in contact with Lois. The number that I had for her—it was disconnected and there was no forwarding number left. And I didn't know a large enough circle of her friends, so I had no way of reaching her. The next time I spoke with her was more than a decade later.

LOIS A few years ago, I was in the AIDS Walk—I do it every year—and I ran into somebody that I went to high school with who is a friend of Patrick's also. And I said, "I lost touch with Pat, do you happen to know . . . ?" Well sure enough, she had his phone number. So I called him. All I said was, "Can I speak to Pat?" and he knew it was me. It was so cool to be talking to him. And then he told me that he and his partner were moving back to Albuquerque—and I was so thrilled!

POSTSCRIPT

"I immediately knew it was her," says Patrick, who was living in Philadelphia at the time with Bart, his partner of seventeen years. "She has an extremely distinctive voice." As it turned out, Lois's partner Anne grew up in Philadelphia and the two were planning a trip there. "The four of us went out to dinner, and we picked up like she had gone on vacation for a week."

Lois did eventually reconcile with her father after he had a heart attack: "I went into the hospital room and I sat down and I just held his hand . . . and he started to cry, and I started to cry. And that's how it happened. He apologized to me, and told me how sorry he was, and that the only thing that meant anything to him was my happiness. And I forgave him, because he's my daddy. And then it was all good from there. He met my partner who, at the time, was Jillian; we were together for almost ten years and then we broke up."

After the break up, Lois tried to make a go of it in Las Vegas, where her parents were living, but "that was, like, total insanity." She did a brief stint in Arizona where she met Anne in 1993, and the couple headed back to Lois's hometown. "It's very cool," says Lois, about being back in Albuquerque. "Seeing people I went to high school and college with—it's almost like I never left."

But she is considering moving again in the next few years. "Actually," notes Patrick, "all four of us are planning to move back to Philadelphia."

The *Mini* Mag

Focus! Focus!

STYLE GUIDES

SEVEN DECADES OF PROM
ACCORDING TO *SEVENTEEN*

SPONSORED BY SCHOOLS, proms have always presented a sanitized version of heterosexual courtship: romantic, not sexual; fun, not debaucherous. And with strict dress codes and Kings and Queens, the event has also promoted the most conservative interpretations of gender.

Perhaps this has been most confining for young women. Uncomfortable as it might be, a guy can throw on a standard-issue tux, buy a corsage, claim boredom, and raise nary a brow. But for the ladies, there are scores of decisions to be made and social mores to navigate.

Since *Seventeen* launched in 1944, its editors have been on hand to offer teens plenty of advice about how to behave and what to wear. Yes, "pretty" and "sweet" are always in style, but a survey of sixty years of *Seventeen* captures subtle and not-so-subtle changes in attitudes and expectations . . .

Merry Manners' mailbag on the great subject of proms

1955

IN THE BEGINNING *SEVENTEEN* TACKLED PROM DILEMMAS LIKE WHETHER OR NOT A GIRL OWES HER DATE A KISS (IT'S OPTIONAL)

2002

THESE DAYS THE MAGAZINE DISCUSSES POST-PROM SEX (IT'S OPTIONAL, TOO) AND GAY COUPLING.

1959

1955

GOOD GIRLS FROM THE MID 1940s THROUGH THE MID 1960s, *SEVENTEEN* PAIRED FAIRY-TALE NOTIONS OF PROM WITH RIGID SOCIAL PROTOCOLS. BACK THEN, WHEN HOME EC WAS A PURELY FEMININE PURSUIT, THE MAGAZINE FEATURED IDEAS FOR "THE PROM BUFFET TABLE" AND DECORATING HOW-TOS. THEN VIETNAM HAPPENED—AND TEENS LIBERATED THEMSELVES.

1962

IS PROM FEVER BACK?

It never went away! Alive, intact and well, the secret of the prom's survival is its simplicity and the desire of many to hold on to old traditions

by Frank Rich

1973

SEX and your BODY

What does it mean to be homosexual?

by Kathy McCoy

According to top sex educators, homosexuality may head the list of sexual anxieties for teenagers. "The fear that you might be homosexual is one of the most common fears of adolescence," says Dr. Sol Gordon, the director of the Institute for Family Research and Education at Syracuse University, in New York. "Many teens fear being homosexual without really knowing what a homosexual is. My definition of a homosexual—which I think a lot of people share—is someone who, *as an adult*, has constant, definite sexual preferences for others of the same sex."

site sex. So experimen...
sex friends first is ...

In fact, according t...
from the American Ac...
atrics, experimentatio...
ual behavior may si...
the route to heteros...
ment. According to...
Kinsey Institute, some...
American men and...
American women ho...
one intentional hom...
ence by the age of fif...
to 20 percent of the p...
mated to be gay. S...
somewhere in betw...
have never responde...

1985

Sex and the prom

The date.

The dress.

The dinner.

The dancing.

The expectations and uncertainties.

The pressure's on— just how will the evening end?

BY JUDITH NEWMAN

1991

MIXED MESSAGES PROM RETURNED WITH A VENGEANCE IN THE MID 1970s. SINCE THEN, *SEVENTEEN*'S READERS DISCOVERED GIRL POWER AND THE MAGAZINE BECAME LESS PRESCRIPTIVE, MORE TOLERANT AND, COME PROM TIME, LOUSY WITH ADS. IN ADDITION TO ITS ANNUAL PROM ISSUE, IN 2003 *SEVENTEEN* BEGAN SELLING A STAND-ALONE "PROM SHOPPING GUIDE."

1976

THE SOFT PROM LOOK is here

2003

real life | my life

i started a gay prom

An alternative to my school's big night.
By Sabrina Smith

SPECIAL PROM SHOPPING ISSUE!

FROM THE WEB

Decade after decade, gay men and women have concocted new ways to handle this heterosexual rite of passage. Finally, there's a place for their stories: www.gayprom.com.

Here's just a few of the highlights from the website. Hopefully, they'll inspire you to post your story. It's totally anonymous . . . unless, of course, you include your prom photo!

FEMALE 1989

Prom was a bit of a blur. Cheesy limo, bad haircuts and lots of satin. I remember that several of the women's dresses had strange hems—short on one side, long on the other. The most memorable gay-related moment came years later when I came out to my date. He was completely unfazed, despite the fact that I had numerous boyfriends before and after him. When I asked him why he wasn't surprised, he recalled that when I was shopping for a prom dress, I was totally outraged that none of dresses came with pockets.

WWW.GAYPROM.COM *KINGS & QUEENS* CONTINUES ONLINE, WHERE YOU CAN POST YOUR PROM STORY AND READ OTHER PEOPLE'S

MALE 1986

My best friend/girlfriend and I lived down the block from each other and I drove to her house real quick to check out her outfit. Before rushing home [to get ready for the prom], I stopped by the beach parking lot and asked a jogger to give me a blowjob. I went home and didn't realize the guy had gone to the police. My father got me out of the shower and told me the police were downstairs and to deny everything. It was never mentioned again.

FEMALE 1964

I attended with a handsome young man who sadly passed away about ten years ago of AIDS. Neither one of us spoke openly of our orientation to the other. I spent the balance of the night at a slumber party stealing a few kisses from the girl who owned my heart at that time. We used no labels back then—we were just in love.

MALE 1979

I had, in my mind, the idea that something wonderful was going to happen to me that night. It was my prom, after all. My date, Cindy, and I were a great combo. We'd won every dance contest offered in the state, and prom was going to be the pinnacle of our "career." Though I had no idea at the time, she was hoping for much more than she would ever get from me. Why? I had my eyes on Marty, the dark-haired football player who never acknowledged my existence.

At the dance, I got quite drunk on Mogen David 20/20 plum wine, six bottles of which were hidden under the front seat of my car. Prom was over by ten p.m. We progressed to Cindy's house for the after-prom party. I kept downing beer and wine with reckless abandon, and before long, my inhibitions were sufficiently lowered enough to find myself in a dark bedroom by myself.

The bedroom door opened and two people entered: Marty and another girl from our class . . . not his date. They plopped down on the bed nearby and began making out. When they fell back onto the mattress, I saw my chance, and fell with them, groping Marty furtively in the dark. It was wonderful, if only for those few seconds that it happened. Of course, I was "outed" in the most tremendous manner a few days later, being kidnapped by a few of the burlier seniors, stripped, spray-painted in the school colors with the word "fag" in white across my chest. I was duct-taped to a speed limit sign on the side of the highway, where I was forced to stay until the police came to rescue me an hour later.

That pristine moment in a dark bedroom with the man of my lusty dreams was what catapulted me into gayhood. Even now, nearly 24 years later, I can feel the texture of his pants beneath my fingers and his hardness as he wrestled with the girl he'd brought into the room with him. Since then, I've embraced my homosexuality in the most fabulous ways . . . and have never regretted one moment of who I am, or who I'm becoming.

FEMALE 2002

My girlfriend and I went to our senior prom together. We were the cutest couple there. We had sex under the bleachers. Our principal found us. It was a great night. =)

Focus! Focus!

QUEER THEMES

For many lesbians, gays, bisexuals and trans teens, the most attractive part of high school is finishing up. In many cases, prom is the last hurdle. And while themes like "Romance in Bloom," "A Walk Down Memory Lane" and "Let's Get It On" suggest what might be on the minds of straight prom goers, the following themes—heavy on escape, transformation and show tunes—suggest the handiwork of those prom committee stalwarts: gay men.

Can you spot some queer messages amid the glitter?

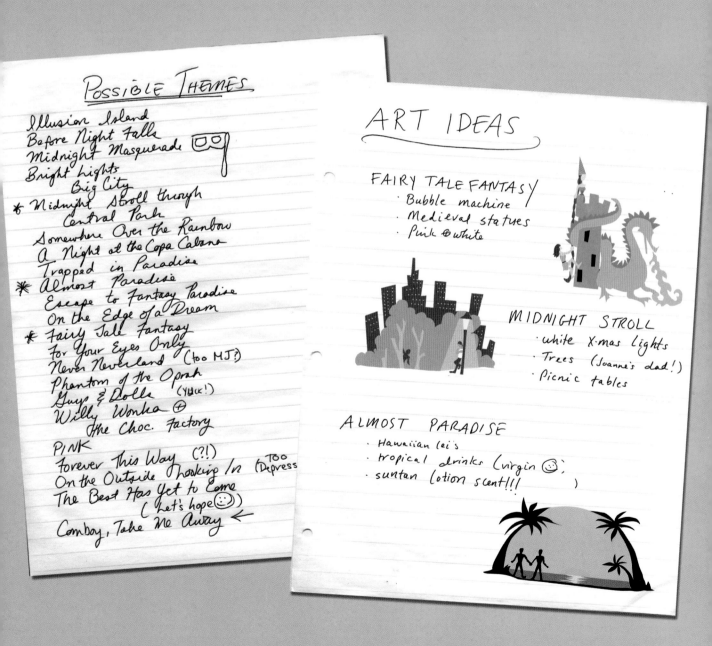

POSSIBLE THEMES

Illusion Island
Before Night Falls
Midnight Masquerade
Bright Lights
    Big City
* Midnight Stroll through
    Central Park
Somewhere Over the Rainbow
A Night at the Copa Cabana
Trapped in Paradise
* Almost Paradise
Escape to Fantasy Paradise
On the Edge of a Dream
* Fairy Tale Fantasy
For Your Eyes Only
Never Neverland (too MJ?)
Phantom of the Oprah
Guys & Dolls (YUCK!)
Willy Wonka &
    The Choc. Factory

PINK
Forever This Way (?!)
On the Outside Looking In (TOO Depress)
The Best Has Yet to Come
    (Let's hope ☺)
Calgary, Take Me Away ←

ART IDEAS

FAIRY TALE FANTASY
· Bubble machine
· Medieval statues
· Pink & white

MIDNIGHT STROLL
· White X-mas lights
· Trees (Joanne's dad!)
· Picnic tables

ALMOST PARADISE
· Hawaiian lei's
· tropical drinks (virgin ☺)
· suntan lotion scent!!!

FOREIGN EXCHANGE

HOW THEY PROM IN THE REST OF THE WORLD

Having clogged foreign airwaves for years with non-stop episodes of *90210* and *The Brady Bunch*, it's not altogether surprising that teens all over the map are familiar with the American prom. And while prom-style parties are becoming more commonplace, most countries have their own graduation traditions. Fortunately for queer teens elsewhere, these celebrations rarely focus on couples and courtship.

UNITED KINGDOM THOSE ABOUT TO GRADUATE ARE CALLED "LEAVERS" AND THE END-OF-THE-YEAR DANCE IS NAMED THE "LEAVERS' BALL." WHILST SOME GO IN COUPLES, THE BALL IS MORE OF A LAST HURRAH FOR THE CLASS. OF COURSE, AS BRITISH SCHOOLING BECOMES MORE AMERI-CANIZED—PRIME MINISTER BLAIR ADVOCATED FOR AMERICAN-STYLE GRADUATION CERE-MONIES—SO DOES THE LEAVERS' BALL, WHICH SOME SCHOOLS NOW CALL "LEAVERS' PROMS."

CANADA THEY CALL THEM "GRADS," BUT THEY CLOSELY RESEMBLE PROMS IN STYLE AND SUBSTANCE, WITH CLICHÉD THEMES, DATES, BALL-ROOMS AND HEAVY DRINKING, FOLLOWED BY A TRIP TO THE BUSH OR THE BEACH. EVEN IN A COUNTRY THAT LEGALIZED GAY MARRIAGE, SAME-SEX COUPLES SOMETIMES RAISE EYEBROWS (AND LAWSUITS). IN 2002, MARC HALL SUED HIS CATHOLIC SCHOOL FOR THE RIGHT TO BRING HIS BOYFRIEND. HE WON!

ITALY *CENTO GIORNI* OR "HUNDRED DAYS" IS THE ITALIAN VERSION OF PROM. SENIORS BEGIN FUNDRAISING ONE-HUNDRED DAYS BEFORE GRADUATION TO PAY FOR A CELEBRATION. "FROM PANHANDLING COINS TO HITTING UP TEACHERS AND OTHER STUDENTS—EVERYTHING GOES," EXPLAINS LUCA, WHO RAISED 200 DOL-LARS (US) FOR HIS. SOME CLASSES USE THE MONEY FOR A DINNER AT A FANCY RESTAURANT, OTHERS ORGANIZE A TRIP—THE DECISION IS LEFT TO THE GRADUATING CLASS.

MEXICO *BAILE DE GRADUACIÓN* LOOKS SIMILAR TO PROM: ATTIRE TENDS TO BE FORMAL AND THE EVENING IS SPENT EATING, DRINKING AND DANC-ING. BUT, AS IN MOST LATIN AMERICAN COUNTRIES, THE PARTY IS A FAMILY AFFAIR. "HERE THE FAMILY ALWAYS IS IN THESE BIG EVENTS," EXPLAINS FERNANDO FROM MEXICO CITY. "YOU CAN GO AS A COUPLE, BUT IN THE MAJORITY OF THE CASES, YOU GO WITH YOUR FAMILY AND FRIENDS, SO THAT WAY IT IS EASIER TO INVITE A BOYFRIEND."

VENEZUELA *CARABANA* BEGINS WHEN THE LAST DAY OF SCHOOL ENDS. STUDENTS HOP INTO CARS DECORATED IN SCHOOL COLORS AND DRIVE AROUND BEEPING THEIR HORNS AND SCREAMING. THAT EVENING, THEY RECONVENE WITH FAMILY, FRIENDS AND TEACHERS AT A FANCY HOTEL FOR A *FIESTA DE GRADUACIÓN*. DATES ARE ALLOWED, BUT NOT REQUIRED.

TRINIDAD & TOBAGO SCHOOLS ORGANIZE GRADUATION PARTIES. "NO ONE HAS TO BE CON-CERNED WITH BRINGING A DATE," SAYS LIVIA, WHO NOW LIVES IN NEW YORK. "YOU JUST SHOW UP LOOKING SUPER FABULOUS AND HANG OUT WITH FRIENDS OR HOOK UP WITH SOMEONE YOU'VE BEEN EYEING FOR THE LAST SEMESTER."

 **FINLAND** IN THEIR FINAL YEAR, STUDENTS ARE CEREMONIOUSLY KICKED OUT DURING A WEEK OF FESTIVITIES. THE CULMINATION IS *VANHOJEN PÄIVIEN TANSSIT*, "DANCE OF THE OLD," A BALL FOR SECOND-YEAR STUDENTS, NOW THE SCHOOL'S ELDEST. WHILE US PROMS CELEBRATE CURRENT FASHION AND MUSIC, THIS AFFAIR PAYS HOMAGE TO THE PAST: BOYS WEAR BLACK TAIL-COATS, GIRLS DON REPLICAS OF CENTURIES-OLD GOWNS. AND THEY PAIR UP FOR TRADITIONAL DANCES PRACTICED THROUGHOUT THE YEAR IN GYM CLASS. WITH PARENTS AND TEACHERS LOOKING ON, IT'S MORE ABOUT PERFORMANCE THAN ROMANCE.

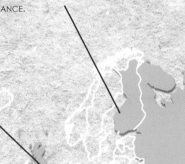 **RUSSIA** AS SOON AS THE POWERS-THAT-BE ANNOUNCE WHO'S PASSED FINAL EXAMS, *VYPUSKNOY VECHER* BEGINS. THE FESTIVITIES INCLUDE A DINNER WHERE GRADUATES DRINK ALCOHOL FOR THE FIRST TIME (OFFICIALLY, AT LEAST) AND LATE-NIGHT DANCING AT A DISCO. AS OPPOSED TO COUPLING, STUDENTS TRAVEL IN PACKS AND TOP OFF THE NIGHT WITH A NOISY, DRUNKEN STROLL THROUGH TOWN CALLED *VSTRECHAT' RASSVET* ("MEET THE SUNRISE"). THE DESTINATION: A MONUMENT WITH A VIEW WHERE THEY WATCH THE SUN RISE TOGETHER BEFORE HEADING TO BED.

 JAPAN AFTER THE GRADUATION CEREMONY, STUDENTS AND PARENTS THANK THE TEACHERS WITH A DINNER PARTY CALLED *SYAONKAI*, WHICH MEANS "GRATITUDE." REMARKED ONE YOUNG JAPANESE WOMAN, "WE DON'T DANCE. NO KISS. NO DRAMATIC EVENT WITH BOYFRIEND. IT'S VERY INNOCENT . . . IN OTHER WORDS: VERY BORING!"

 SOUTH AFRICA THE MATRIC DANCES OF SOUTH AFRICA ARE PRACTICALLY IDENTICAL TO PROM. DATES ARE EXPECTED, BUT LESS EMPHASIS IS PLACED ON ROMANCE AND SEX.

 **KUWAIT** "WE DON'T HAVE ANYTHING LIKE WHAT WE SEE ON TV ABOUT THESE PARTIES IN YOUR COUNTRY. IT IS JUST ORDINARY, WITHOUT ANY HARM TO ANYTHING . . . JUST JOKE, TALK AND EAT," EXPLAINS A YOUNG MAN ABOUT KUWAITI GRADUATIONS CALLED *TAKHAREJ*. EVEN THOUGH DANCING IS FROWNED UPON IN PUBLIC, STUDENTS ARE ABLE TO GET DOWN AT PRIVATE PARTIES—SOME CO-ED, SOME SINGLE SEX—IN RESTAURANTS, RENTED VILLAS OR UNDER HUTS NEAR THE BEACH, A.K.A. *CHALEH*.

 **ZIMBABWE** HANGING ONTO ITS COLONIAL HERITAGE, ZIMBABWE'S EDUCATIONAL SYSTEM MIRRORS THE UK'S, RIGHT DOWN TO A LEAVERS' BALL. THE BIG DIFFERENCE FOR GAYS: HOMOSEXUALITY IS ILLEGAL HERE AND, IF CONVICTED, OPENLY GAY PEOPLE (A.K.A. *MOFFIES*) CAN BE JAILED FOR UP TO FIFTEEN YEARS.

 ISRAEL A DECADE AGO, HIGH SCHOOL GRADUATION WAS MARKED WITH FAMILIAL PARTIES AND SCHOOL ACTIVITIES; ONE WOMAN REMEMBERS HER CLASS HIRING A DIRECTOR AND WRITING AN ORIGINAL SHOW, WHICH WAS PERFORMED FOR FRIENDS AND RELATIVES. NOW IT'S ALL ABOUT PROM: TUXES, BALLROOMS AND THE REST ARE BECOMING THE NORM.

 AUSTRALIA WHILE THEY ATTEND A PROM-STYLE DANCE AT THE END OF SCHOOL, GRADUATES (OR "LEAVERS") ARE REALLY LOOKING FORWARD TO WHAT FOLLOWS: "SCHOOLIES WEEK," A PARTY ON THE GOLD COAST THAT ATTRACTS 50,000 LEAVERS FROM ALL OVER THE COUNTRY. IT HAS GROWN SO ROWDY THAT THE GOVERNMENT (WORRIED ABOUT SAFETY), CHURCHES (BRINGING FAITH TO THE DEVIL'S PLAYGROUND), CULTS (HOPING TO SCORE NEW RECRUITS) AND TOURISM COMPANIES (LOOKING TO MAKE GOBS OF MONEY) HAVE ALL GOTTEN IN ON THE ACTION.

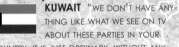

PROM TRENDS

DECADE BY DECADE

Every spring for the past seven decades, millions of high school students head to prom. And each time, teens have to make the same decisions: what to wear, how to get there, and what to do after it's over. While the questions are the same, the choices and trends differ. Except of course, when it comes to flowers: corsages are always in style.

	1940s	1950s	1960s	
MEN'S FASHIONS	zoot suit proportions means oversized tuxes	the classic: white tuxedo jacket and black pants	color enters the picture	
WOMEN'S FASHIONS	dramatic patterns, light colors and full skirts	fitted bodices, full skirts (crinolines rule!)	calling Jackie O: tailored cuts and elegant gloves	
FLOWERS	wrist corsage	wrist corsage	wrist corsage	
MUSIC	orchestras play waltzes and Big Band	orchestras continue to play the classics; rock-and-roll begins to happen	bands indulge in Beatlemania and soulful Motown	
LOCATION	in the gym	in the gym	in the gym	
GETTING THERE	car	car	car	
BEFORE PROM	male picks up female	male picks up female	male picks up female; go to fancy dinner	
AFTER PROM	necking and then home	necking and then home	after-party at someone's home	
VICE OF CHOICE	cigarettes, alcohol	alcohol	alcohol , dope, acid	
QUEER COUPLES	don't even think about it at the prom	nope	nope	

1970s	1980s	1990s	2000s
powder-blue tuxes with lots of ruffles	all white or light gray, right down to the Capezios	simple black or vintage tux, colorful bow ties and vests	suits and tuxes are dark; ties replace bow ties
long, flowy, floral	sequined and strapless; very *Dynasty*	shorter and tighter; longer and slimmer	whatever J. Lo and company are wearing on the red carpet
wrist corsage	wrist corsage	wrist corsage	wrist corsage
bands start the '70s with "Stairway to Heaven"; later disco rules the dance floor	bands mix R&B with metal ballads (think: Journey)	DJs alternate between Nirvana and bubble gum pop	DJs get jiggy with it and have a lot more than one "Moment Like This"
in the gym	gym or hotel ballroom	at a hotel	at a hotel
car	car or limo	limo	stretch SUV
male picks up female; go to fancy dinner	male picks up female; go to fancy dinner	pre-party at friend's house	pre-party at friend's house
after-party at someone's home	after-party at hotel or beach	go away to beach or lake	after-party at school then go away
everything, anything	alcohol, dope, cocaine	alcohol, dope, acid (late night)	alcohol, dope, ecstasy (late night)
almost impossible	unlikely	a few; more likely at gay prom	no longer shocking

MINORITIES REPORT

Gays, lesbians and transgendered teens aren't the only ones sweating prom night. The rite of passage collides with the rules and realities of other minority groups, forcing some to miss the dance and others to obey some thorny restrictions. Buck up queer boys and girls, it could be worse.

1%
MUSLIM

For unmarried Muslims, it's against the rules to date or dance with members of the opposite sex and wear revealing attire in their presence, which strikes at the core of the typical prom.

While most Muslim teens avoid the night altogether, groups of Muslim girls in the United States and Canada have begun to organize "dateless" proms, (ignoring the probability of lesbians in their midst). According to Leslie Scrivener, who covered one for the *Toronto Star*, the young women "arrived cocooned in hijab, the Islamic headscarf, and long jackets. But once in the safety of the hall, they revealed strapless dresses, beaded halter-top gowns" and danced to pop and rap music spun by two female DJs.

One Muslim girl who went to her school's prom, discussed her experience on a community bulletin board: "I wore my hijab and I was fully covered . . . and I was not the only muslimah in attendance . . . their [sic] were many of us who went and we had a GREAT time and it was all very fun and clean."

1.5%
HOME SCHOOLED

Roughly two million American kids are schooled in their homes. As homeschooling becomes more popular, so does the question "What about prom?" While homeschooling certainly limits the dating pool, parents are increasingly organized—networking online and establishing regional events to fill the void. Not just on prom night, but for sports, science fairs and other extracurricular activities.

Still, since homeschooling is often chosen for religious reasons, prom night tends to be a muted affair. One homeschooler from Oklahoma posted this message on one of the many prom-related websites for teens: "Yes, homeschoolers have prom. But since we're pretty conservative, we don't dance, so it's just Junior-Senior banquet. The best theme I know is 'Stardust' . . . Stardust is really versatile and there are tons of star items out there for cheap. I know because I'm on the comittee [sic] that buys the stuff. God Bless You! Have an awesome prom!"

2%
JEWISH

Some of the more orthodox Jews share similar biblical mandates to Muslims. For instance, they too are "discouraged" from interacting with the opposite sex before marriage. And "mixed dancing," as it's called, is therefore not allowed nor, technically speaking, is touching.

For Jews who keep a kosher diet, prom dinner presents specific challenges. By Jewish law, they cannot eat meat and milk in the same meal nor can they eat meat that comes from pigs. While the vegetarian option works for some, the most orthodox Jews will only eat food that has been supervised by a rabbi and with kosher utensils.

Another issue: proms are often scheduled on Friday nights, part of the sun-down-to-sun-up period of rest called shabbat during which some Jews do not drive. That's the reason orthodox Jew and United States Senator Joseph Lieberman skipped his high school prom, even though his classmates voted him Prom King.

OUT OF
16,000,000
AMERICAN TEENS

8%
GAY

2%
MORMON

In a teen fashion universe obsessed with Britney Spears's belly button and Jennifer Lopez's booty, young Mormon women face a unique challenge: figuring out a way to be both modest and stylish.

To help young Mormon women adhere to their church's rules for dress and appearance, Chris Hash launched ModestProm.com. "My guidelines for ModestProm," explains Chris, "are that dresses must cover the top of the shoulder, be high-cut in front and back, not reveal the midriff, not be too tight, and not have slits that go above the knee."

16%
POOR

More than three million teens are living beneath the poverty level. Many others live in foster homes and families struggling to make ends meet. Prom is no cheap affair; and when it's a question of food for the family or a limo to the dance, you can guess which most parents choose.

Organizations such as Prom Closet in Nevada, the Cinderella Project in New Hampshire and Operation Prom Dress in New York have popped up to outfit a few young women in need. But most go without their dream dress. Many, sadly, don't go at all.

19%
OF COLOR

Another recent and disturbing trend is the return or, in some cases, continuation of the white-only prom. While segregated proms are not the norm, "White Proms" and "Black Proms" are not unheard of in conservative pockets of the South, including parts of Louisiana, Alabama, Mississippi and Georgia.

In 2003, the tradition went public. After holding its first integrated prom in three decades just one year earlier, students of Taylor County High School in Albany, Georgia returned to their old ways. ABC, CNN, FOX and others were on hand to cover the event; and op-ed pages and internet bulletin boards buzzed with disapproval, shock and outrage for weeks.

SOURCES AMERICAN RELIGION DATA ARCHIVE (MUSLIM, JEWISH, MORMON); NATIONAL CENTER FOR EDUCATIONAL STATISTICS (BASED ON ESTIMATE THAT 250,000 TEENS ARE HOMESCHOOLED); US CENSUS, 2000 (AMERICAN TEENS, POOR); AVERAGE OF SEVERAL ESTIMATES (GAYS)

JUNIORS

CLASSMATES GET DOWN AT SUSAN
FORD'S PROM, HELD IN HER FATHER'S
WHITE HOUSE IN **1975**

ILLINOIS IS FIRST STATE TO
DECRIMINALIZE HOMOSEXUALITY
1962

US DEPLOYS TROOPS TO
VIETNAM AND PROTESTS BEGIN
1965

1960
BIRTH CONTROL PILL HITS THE MARKET

1963
MARTIN LUTHER KING, JR. DELIVERS "I HAVE A DREAM" SPEECH

New ideas challenged old ones as Baby Boomers came of age and sparked a cultural revolution.

US PSYCHIATRISTS DROP "HOMOSEXUALITY"
FROM LIST OF DISORDERS
1973

HARVEY MILK BECOMES FIRST OPENLY
GAY MAN ELECTED TO PUBLIC OFFICE
1978

1969
STONEWALL RIOTS ROCK GREENWICH VILLAGE

THE
PORN
STAR

TONY SCALIA

AUSTIN HIGH SCHOOL
DECATUR, ALABAMA
CLASS OF **1979**

He was a reluctant heartthrob from the very beginning—since elementary school, to be precise. "All of the girls were in love with me. They would follow me around or come over and want to buy my shoestrings or whatever," explains the Alabama native who talks to his mom every Sunday.

Although the audience is quite different, Tony is still making hearts race. At the unlikely age of forty-one, he has a burgeoning career in gay adult videos, appearing in more than a dozen films, including *Take It Like a Man*, *Time Cop* and *Pumped Up*.

While his physique has been his ticket to porn demi-stardom, Tony remains surprisingly insecure. "I don't know why people like it," he says. "The first thing I do when somebody gives me the compliment—and I hate myself for doing it—I will turn around and say something negative about my body; I get embarrassed."

"I was a skinny kid," he adds. "And when I look in the mirror, I still see the skinny little arms, the skinny little legs."

I DATED GIRLS IN ELEMENTARY SCHOOL. I would break up with one, go out with another and then break up with her and go out with another. They were all throwing themselves at me.

This went on until junior high, and then I started going through puberty and I wasn't cute and adorable anymore. I got tall and lanky and my hair turned kinky curly.

> "I started going through puberty and I wasn't cute and adorable anymore. I got tall and lanky and my hair turned kinky curly."

In tenth grade, I even had a big afro; I'd put a net on in the morning and get it all nice and round, and then I'd hairspray it. Oh God, that was horrible!

I didn't really have any male friends in high school. The guys, they hated me—called me sissy and all this other stuff. I was pretty much a loner, but I was on the cross-country team and I roller-skated.

This was during the whole roller disco era. I entered all of these local contests. My partner was Sharon. We were good: we made it all the way to a national contest sponsored by Coca Cola and placed second in couples. We were on the news and there were articles in the newspaper about us. So, a lot of people in high school knew about it, but they weren't really into it.

All through high school, I didn't feel like I belonged. I knew something was going on; I just wasn't connecting with all of these other people. I knew I was different, but because of where I grew up, I didn't know about being gay. All I knew was feeling an attraction to another guy was wrong. But I did play around with other guys in high school, you know. And I knew I liked that—with girls I never had any desire.

Because I really wasn't friends with any girls from my school, I couldn't find anyone to go with to prom. There was this one girl that I really had a crush on. I asked her, but she wouldn't go with me. She said she *would* date me, but not until after high school. She was a cheerleader and she thought I only wanted to go with her because she was popular, which was probably true. I don't think it ever crossed my mind to invite Sharon: we were skating partners and close friends, but had totally separate social lives.

Luckily, there was a nineteen-and-under dance club in Florence, Alabama—about forty miles from Decatur. I used to go there with some women I worked with at a men's clothing store. There was this really beautiful girl at the club who I would dance with a lot. And so I ended up asking her.

The night of the prom we went to the Cellar, which was this really nice restaurant at the airport, and we had this fabulous seven-course meal. Then we went to the prom. It used to be in the gymnasium, but that year they moved it to the cafeteria. Tacky. You have all those windows all around and a low ceiling.

I wore a brown tux to the junior prom, because my date was wearing beige. But I wore a white tux to the senior prom, because I had no idea what color my date's dress would be. She ended up wearing lime green, and everyone told her she had such a beautiful dress.

I didn't really want to go, but I felt like I had to: I didn't want to feel like a loser.

I didn't really want to go, but I felt like I had to: I didn't want to feel like a loser. I already felt like an outsider and, it was just, you know, I was just trying to feel like I belonged. But I felt uncomfortable the whole night. Part of it was having someone from out of town; part of it was being insecure, feeling like none of the girls that knew me from high school wanted to go with me. I think I even pointed out the girl I asked out first to my date.

After the prom, I had to drive her all the way back to Florence. I felt like she wanted me to do something. She always wanted me to do something; at the dance club, sometimes afterwards, we'd sit in the car together and kiss. I always felt like she wanted me to make a move, but it didn't appeal to me. And when I dropped her off on prom night, I just gave her a kiss and that was it.

I didn't feel sexual in high school—asexual maybe—I was petrified of it. I couldn't imagine being naked in front of people. I mean, I weighed 140-something pounds when I graduated. Now I weigh 180. That's why I'm surprised when people from high school recognize me. To me, I don't look anything the same. My nose is probably bigger since my hair's further back. I don't know what stayed the same, because it's *not* the body.

TOP TONY WITH SHARON AT A ROLLER DISCO COMPETITION
ABOVE TONY IN NINTH GRADE **RIGHT** TONY WITH AFRO
PREVIOUS PAGES TONY AT THE PROM; SIXTH GRADE PHOTO

NEW ENGLAND SUMMER

When I watched
my video, that was
the first time
I realized what my
body looked like.

THIS WEEK
IN TEXAS
September 26 –
October 2, 1997

DANCE
The Houston
Ballet Presents
Cinderella

What's Out of
Interest to
Gay People

CURRENT EVENT
STARSCOPE
BACKSTAGE
TEXAS NEWS

LEFT TONY ON HIS FIRST VIDEO BOX INSET ON THE COVER OF *TWIT* (THIS WEEK IN TEXAS)
ABOVE WITH MOM ON CHRISTMAS, 1997

I started working out heavily after I broke up with a guy I had been dating for four years. And I ended up on the cover of a gay bar rag. And this agent from L.A. saw the picture and contacted me and asked if I'd be interested in doing photo work or a video. And I said, "Maybe photo work, but I don't think I can do a video." So he asked me a couple more times. Eventually, I said, "Well, why don't you just check around?" I mean, I didn't think anyone would want me. He called me a week later with four offers and asked if I wanted to do it. So I asked my friends, and everyone's like, "Yeah, do it. I would." So I did.

When I watched *The Dirty Director*, my video that just came out, that was the first time I realized what my body looked like. I saw it and I was like, *Wow*. I didn't realize I was that big. Like right now, I feel like a skinny little kid. But then when I saw myself on the screen—maybe I was with a smaller guy—but I looked huge. I was kind of in awe. I watched it a couple of times—not for the sex, but to figure out, Is that really me?

I don't think my prom date would be surprised to find out I'm gay—it would probably answer a lot of questions. But I don't know how she would react to knowing I do porn, because I know it's totally different to gay people than it is to straight people. Because in gay life, porn stars aren't looked down on. It's kind of like a pedestal. People are like, "Oh my God, I met a porn star." You feel like you're a chosen one. But you hear a lot of things about how straight porn victimizes women. I don't feel like a victim; I'm having a damn good time. I'm getting paid to have sex with good-looking guys. What more could you ask for?

I think it's neat, like I just came out on a box cover, which was my first box cover, and it was a really good picture and I was like, *Whoa!* And when I go out of town, it's kind of neat to get recognized. Because people come up to you and are like, "I saw you in so and so." I've even run into a few people from high school who turned out to be gay, and they think it's cool. But it can also be kind of embarrassing, especially if it's a video you thought you looked horrible in.

It's weird, I never felt like I fit in, in high school. And I still don't feel like I fit in with the gay community. Maybe that's one of the reasons I do videos. To be accepted. It's hard to explain, it's just a feeling I have.

"I was actually planning on going to my twenty-fifth reunion, but now I'm getting a little nervous," says Tony. "I'm starting to get more and more known, so I don't know. I don't want to do anything that's going to embarrass my mother. And Decatur is a small, religious town. I'm sure the people who still live there would be horrified to find out that I do porn. Especially gay porn."

"It surprises me a little bit that I'm still doing porn in my forties. I don't know how much longer it's going to last," adds Tony, who had an emergency hip-replacement surgery in 1999. "That's why I'm trying to do as much of it as I can right now."

Recently, his doctor advised him to reduce the amount of weight he lifts with his legs from 600 pounds to 400, because he's wearing out the now-artificial cartilage too quickly. "I didn't react well," he admits. "Because when I do less weight, it feels like I'm not doing anything. So I'm a little stressed about that. My legs are pretty good, but they're not quite where I want them to be."

Tony's trying to figure out what he'll do once adult videos are no longer an option. "I've been thinking a lot about that lately," he says. "I would like to get a full-time job with a steady income."

THE
NEW
GIRL

JENNY BOYLAN

HAVERFORD HIGH SCHOOL
DEVON, PENNSYLVANIA
CLASS OF **1976**

She was born James, was called Jim by friends, but always felt like Jenny. "I knew from age three that I was female—that I should be a girl. I didn't understand that I wasn't going to grow up to be a woman," explains the author of the witty, insightful memoir, *She's Not There: A Life in Two Genders.*

In fact, he did grow up to be a woman. In 1999 James, already married with two children, began his transition to Jenny, finally uniting body with soul.

Prom date and friend Sarah O'Brien was somewhat surprised by the change, but completely supportive. "The sense I had of Jim was that he was not a sexual being," says Sarah. "I'm sure he was, but because he was smart and funny, he was sort of the clown. And he managed to find a group of people who really valued him for who he was. So they weren't thinking, Why isn't Jim going on more dates? Why isn't he more macho?"

JENNY

> "I would usually go upstairs and put on a skirt and do my homework. Because it was just easier to concentrate if I was cross-dressed."

BY THE TIME I WAS IN HIGH SCHOOL, I knew exactly how much trouble I was in. Here I am, this young transgendered person, going to an all-male prep school in one of the most conservative parts of the country, which was a nightmare that was so hilarious that a lot of the time I just kind of floated above the whole thing, like it was an absurd dream.

Most days I would come home from school around four o'clock. I would spend about a half hour reading the comics and eating a Hostess cupcake, drinking a glass of milk. Then I'd play the piano for about an hour and I would just kind of free-associate, in a kind of wild Grateful Dead, John Coltrane jam. After that, I would usually go upstairs and put on a skirt and hose, which I'd steal from my sister, and lock my bedroom door and do my homework. Because it was just easier to concentrate if I was cross-dressed. It wasn't an erotic act; it was an act of relief.

My sister's clothes were all Grateful Dead clothes, and those were my fashions, too. There were little peasant blouses with little mirrors sewn into them. Or Danskin leotards. What's actually bizarre is that more than twenty years later, when I went through transition, I essentially picked up my fashion sense right where I'd left off in adolescence. I went through three or four months of wearing

I called up Sarah and I said, "Look, I just can't deal with this whole prom thing. Would you just go with me?"

hippie clothes from the '70s before I realized this was all very, very wrong. I can't be teaching my classes in a peasant blouse with little mirrors sewn onto it.

I never had a moment really when I didn't know "it" was there. But here's what transsexuals do: you start making these deals with yourself, that it'll be okay if . . . I always believed that if only I were loved by a woman that I would be content to be a man. I tried; I had girlfriends, but it would never last. I'd go out on a date and I'd ask questions like, "What's it like to have breasts?" It was all about trying to get as close to these girls as possible, because if I couldn't be myself, I could at least be of them, among them. But it wasn't what women wanted on a date.

There was one girl who I had an obsession with. Let's call her Rachel. And I just adored her and wanted to take her to the prom. She went to another one of the prep schools. In a way Rachel was an example of the kind of woman I wanted to be: she wasn't overly feminine; she was smart, she was funny and, above all, she had a sense of dignity and self-respect. Rachel didn't particularly want to date me. She wanted to be my friend. So when I asked her to the prom, she said, "Yeah, I'll go with you, but only if this isn't some big date." I said, "Okay."

Well, then I met this other woman. Let's call her Mary. And Mary was a girl who *was* attracted to me, so I asked her if she'd go to the prom. And then I called Rachel back and said that I couldn't go with her—and that was fine by her.

TOP JIM IN TYPICAL SCHOOL ATTIRE, FALL OF 1975 BOTTOM ON SENIOR C DAY RIGHT SARAH AT JIM'S PROM PREVIOUS PAGES HELPING THEMSELVES PROM; JIM BLOWING UP BALLOONS FOR HIS EIGHTH-BIRTHDAY PARTY; PLAY GUITAR, CIRCA 1975

So, here I am with Mary and I'm, like, falling in love with her. It was what I had longed for throughout my whole adolescence, for that moment. But when it finally came to me, I couldn't rise to the occasion; I was afraid that I would be a failure with her, that she would somehow see that I was a woman on the inside and that would turn her off, to say the least. Or she would be able to see that I had some deep secret that I couldn't share with her and I would be this person who was fundamentally unknowable. It just seemed impossible. So I called her up, and I think I told her that I was having this after-prom party at my house and I was going to be too busy to have a date that night. She sounded unbelievably disappointed and crushed.

Now it is like a week before the prom and I've had these two separate girls who I'm in love with, and I'm realizing at this moment that I'm never really going to be able to really have the courage to be in love with anybody. So I called up my friend Sarah and I said, "Look, I just can't deal with this whole prom thing. Would you just go with me?" And she said, "Of course, it'd be great."

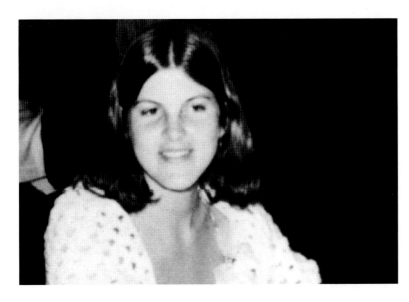

SARAH Jim was great. He was very, very smart, very funny, sort of Monty Python. He would improvise jazz on the piano, sing songs like "Here's to You Mr. Coffee" and "Here's to You Mrs. Robinson." He and I would hang out, joke around, go out on the roof outside his room with star charts and look for Scorpio, and just have a really great time together.

I think it must have been awkward for him to be *so* in that boy culture and to get to that dating phase and not necessarily be in that framework, not thinking about things in the same way. He was not a dating kind of guy; he was not the guy that you thought, Ooh, I'm going to have a crush on him. He was somebody who was happy being in the crowd—not the big macho crowd, but the smaller crowd of us that really laughed and smoked pot and hung out and just enjoyed each other's company.

I was probably on the butch end of the spectrum for girls, and he to the femmy end of the spectrum for the boys, so we kind of met in the middle in a very comfortable way. Being asked by Jim was kind of perfect. I thought, Oh great, I can go to the prom with somebody who I just really have a fun time with. And, you know, we didn't have to pretend to be in love.

JENNY In this kind of "society culture" that we grew up in, we would go to these debutante balls, supposedly with our tongues in cheek. We'd get absolutely as high as we could and then walk through these doors unable to talk. The next thing we know, Jeeves is handing us an antique champagne glass. I must have gone to maybe three or four when I was in tenth grade, and maybe six of them when I was a junior, maybe ten of them when I was a senior. So in some ways the prom was less of a big deal than going to someone's coming-out party.

Also, the whole culture of the prom has changed a lot since 1976: we didn't have any of the stuff like driving around in limos; I just met Sarah at a party at my friend Mark's house. And she looked great, she looked just gorgeous. She was wearing this great dress with flowers on it. And, of course, my immediate thought was, Shit, I'd look good in that.

After Mark's, we all drove over to the prom, which was only about a mile or two away at this place called the Covered Wagon. There wasn't like a theme, that was too tacky. Since we belonged to this insane little culture, we missed out on the essential tackiness of the prom: we didn't have the giant baked-bean volcano or the girl dressed up in the hula skirt. There were probably tasteful sprays of orchids and irises all over the place. Looking at it now, it's like something out of the '20s, something out of Fitzgerald.

After the prom, there was a party at my house. So here we are, all standing around in our tuxedos. And there was a keg of beer; I'm sure there were people smoking pot somewhere. At some point, maybe it was like two o'clock in the morning, Sarah turned to me and she said, "I think I'm going to head home now." I remember looking at her and for the first time feeling this profound sorrow, because I felt, I bet I've disappointed her, too. I also knew that she was going to leave and my prom night was going to end without

I called my high school and told the alumni that I wanted to be taken off their rolls. And they said, "Why?"

RIGHT COLBY COLLEGE IDS, BEFORE AND AFTER
FAR RIGHT JIM IN FLORENCE, ITALY, 1999
OPPOSITE PAGE THE COVER OF JENNY'S BOOK

even a kind of fake hug and a kiss from the girl that I'd taken, because I was too scared and too confused to even do that. So I was sad for her, but I was also sad for me.

I spent the rest of the night hanging out with my other friends. But I was aware that I hadn't had this classic mythological experience. And people who think of their prom as this "great night," I think it's because their experience matched mythology. And I was aware at that time that mine didn't. Still, I look back on it with incredible gratefulness and joy and love because, what can I say, you can't spend your whole life being bitter. Look, I was a transgendered woman. In 1970, who knew what that was? But I had all these good friends. We went out, we danced, we stayed up so late. And, twenty-seven years later, the woman that I went with is still a good friend. When she found out that I was changing genders, she said to me, "Good for you, I'm proud of you." So, why shouldn't I be glad?

SARAH He sent this wonderful Christmas letter after he had gone through, I guess, the final change. And, oh it's a great letter, all about his son swallowing a marble. They had to search through his shit and look for this thing to make sure that it had passed through him. Jim ended up

using this as a metaphor for how life had been for a little while—it was like searching through the shit and finding this treasure.

So, I'm a reading this thing about the shit and the marble and suddenly it's like, "And I'm Jenny now." And it's like, *Wow! Whoa!* Because I had not been close enough to them while it was happening to hear about it. But I was just so astounded and pleased at the idea that he and Grace and their family had been able to go through this whole thing together—it just seemed like a miracle. And I could see, I mean I can't say, "Oh yeah, I always thought he was a girl." But I could easily say, "Sure, I could see where, you know, he could have gone either way and I guess he felt a really strong leaning in this direction." What really was funny was their return address label said, "Jenny and Grace Boylan." And I had looked at it and I thought,

Huh, that's funny. And just sort of set it aside and went on to read the letter. And then I got to the end and thought, *Oh*, I get it. So it seemed like a great resolution to something that has clearly been difficult or problematic for years.

There aren't that many people from high school that I keep up with. But I would bet that a lot of people, who are still there doing their plaid pants and cocktails—I bet it freaked them right out. Although when I go back there, I'm always intrigued by their ability to adjust to other concepts or deal with things you would think are way out of their range. Because I've lived a very different life than most of those people. I mean, I've been gay, I've been straight, I've been in New York, I've done film, I've been poor, I've traveled around to all different places and I haven't done the things the way they do them. But they're so confident. They're wealthy people, their families have been wealthy people for 200 years, and they feel very unthreatened. So in some ways, even though their actual politics may be conservative about money, their ability to kind of take in different ways of being is often very great. In some ways, I think because a lot of them are very privileged people, they have a certain—it's not openness like, "Oh yeah, I'd do that too." But it's openness like, "Huh, wow, kudos Jim." And also, there's that old school-ties sort of thing, like, "Well he's one of ours."

JENNY After I went through transition, I called my high school and told the alumni that I wanted to be taken off their rolls, that it just didn't make any sense for me to be still getting the alumni newsletter and everything from the school. And they said, "Why?" And I said, "Well, because I'm a transsexual." And they said to me, "Well Jennifer, what makes you think you're the only transsexual that went to the Haverford School? There are several transsexuals who went here and, in fact, a member of the class of '62, who was on the crew team, had a gender shift ten years ago. And she still comes back and rows with the crew team." Still, I haven't been to any reunions. For one thing, I think I was having my surgery during the twenty-fifth. Literally.

My experience of seeing people has been almost uniformly great; people have been kind and compassionate and generous to me. But the people who have the hardest time are A) men and B) people who knew me a long time ago as a guy. So, I'm thinking that if I go back to one of those reunions, I'm likely to run into a group of people with the highest percentage of both of those things.

Also, in retrospect, it was a very painful time. I was saved not only by friendships, but also by a kind of buoyancy and optimism that I inherited from my mother. But, boy, it took gallons and gallons of optimism to get me through that time in my life, and it's not a place I particularly want to revisit.

"I don't have any regrets about anything other than the trauma that my transition has caused the people I love," says Jenny, who married Grace in 1988. "I feel like I've had this wonderful gift: that I've been able to see into two worlds. And, quite frankly, my life as James was delightful and very blessed. I had a great marriage, I have a wonderful family, a good job—all that stuff. If I could have kept on being James forever I would have."

"That thing I'd always hoped for—being truly and deeply loved by a woman—is something that finally happened to me," explains Jenny about the relationship with Grace. "And what I learned in the end was that even *that* was not enough to make this untrue. I'm a transsexual. I had to deal with it, I dealt with it, and I was lucky enough to come through it. And isn't this one of the things we do with our lives? We try to take the thing that is our greatest curse and make it into our greatest blessing. And I guess that's what I've tried to do. In many ways, I'm very, very grateful to have been given this gift. It's a rich life and I've seen some really amazing things."

SHE'S NOT THERE
A LIFE IN TWO GENDERS

JENNIFER FINNEY BOYLAN
With an Afterword by Richard Russo

HIGH SCHOOL
SWEETHEARTS

DAVID PACE & BOB MOON

HOOVER HIGH SCHOOL
NORTH CANTON, OHIO
CLASS OF **1973**

"It is odd," admits David Pace (on the left), who met his partner, architect Bob Moon, in 1969, "I married my high school sweetheart."

The two, born toward the end of the Baby Boom, grew up in what Bob describes as "an all-white town that's very conservative in its thinking, predominantly Republican, predominantly German and predominantly Protestant."

Together, they have lived through the Vietnam War and the sexual revolution, AIDS and disco, thickening waistlines and, yes, the prom.

"I can't even imagine if Bob and I had gone our separate ways," says David, a graphic artist and creative director, "because who I am is so much a part of being involved with him . . . Maybe I'd be a famous opera singer."

DAVID I SAW HIM THAT FIRST DAY of Miss Neglucci's art class. He sat with his friends from Catholic school at one table; and I was with the more outré people. We hit it off right away, even though we were sitting at opposite ends of the room. Then we ended up sitting at the same lunch table.

BOB HE WALKED IN AND I HAD A HUGE CRUSH. At the time, I didn't know what the hell to do about it. Because it was so unexpected. And what are you going to do about it in an environment that curses it?

So we became best friends. We had a really ideal, fabulous relationship before it was ever physical. First of all, the thing that bound us to one another most tightly was a commonality of thought: we were interested in the same things; we took the same art classes; and we were in the same little singing group. So we did all that stuff together.

We actually went all through high school before we consummated our relationship. And we didn't even discuss it until senior year.

DAVID It's hard to understand, but you just didn't couch things in those terms— not in the Midwest in the 1970s. It was very tentative. But I think certain people are meant to be together, and they will be together.

You know, I was always very subtle about it, but I think I was a little more aggressive in pursuing the whole thing. I just kind of zeroed in and thought, Huh, this is a great guy; he's hot. So we'll see where this goes.

I pursued him just by being around and hanging out with the same people. And in high school, it was things like, "Hey let's go water-skiing . . . and let's go naked."

I think people always suspected there was something going on. They knew—there was, like, tension. And, yeah, there was talk, especially the girls, saying things like, "Why are they always hanging out together?" But what were they going to do about it? They couldn't find photos of us butt-fucking.

BOB Of course, we went to the prom together—we did everything together. I just thought prom was stupid, but if we had to do it, we might as well do it together.

We double dated: David went with Judy Lukens, and Jody Matthie was my date. I went with her because she was a really pretty, lovely, nice girl—and we weren't looking to find a girl to marry or lay. I mean, it was not this nasty case of using her just to spend the evening with him; that's just who I wanted to go with. Jody and I had respect for one another and enjoyed one another, and we were just going to go and have a good time.

Really, the evening was pretty unexceptional. I've forgotten a lot, because, you know, I didn't wear my glasses that night. But I suppose, if you want to get all dewey-eyed about it, I can remember dancing with my date and thinking, I wish I was dancing with David. And I remember what he wore: that brown suit.

> **DAVID** There was talk, especially the girls. But what were they going to do about it? They couldn't find photos of us butt-fucking.

DAVID That was the year of really, really hideous tuxes; we're talking about powder-blue velvet tuxedos. No way was I going to wear that. In fact, we both wore suits, which was really pioneering. Bob's suit was blue with a little bit of white; it was polyester. And Jody had made her dress herself—she was crowned something like the Queen of Future Farmers—and she made him a tie that matched her dress.

We picked them up and went to this famous supper club in Akron called Tangiers. After Ike Turner beat Tina up and threw her out, Tangiers was one of the only places that would give her a job. And Tangiers had this restaurant, which of all things, was Lebanese.

We got to the prom around nine. It was in the gym. The art students always did the decorations, but it was always the Junior Art Club that did it, not the seniors; so I worked on it the year before. And you would go through these catalogues; you bought a floor to cover the basketball court and crepe-paper ceilings that you would hoist up to the gym ceiling—it's a whole industry. I can't remember the theme our senior year, but I remember the year before it was "A Trip to China." It was red and black; it looked like a Chinese whorehouse. And I spent thousands of hours recreating the Ming Dynasty on rice paper.

Anyway, we were at the prom until eleven. Then we dumped the girls off—which was the correct thing to do—and we drove around for hours by ourselves in Bob's father's midnight-blue Buick Electra. And the first time we kissed—it was in that car. Boy, that was a little seduction machine; the backseat was as wide as a sofa.

BOB But we were really, really guarded and defensive. We had to be; if you ventured into that in any open way, you could be beaten to an inch of your life. And both of our families are kind, but they come from conservative, religious backgrounds. Had we been found out, there's a really good chance that the knee-jerk reaction would have been, "Get out of our house."

Still, it's not like we were just celibate little boys. In fourth grade I had this hot thing going with a friend of mine. It went on for a while, then it stopped. Then in eighth grade we had these giant orgies, and he and I were always with one another. Then there was like a two-year hiatus, and one night it was just like *bang!*

RIGHT BACKGROUND DAVID (IN THE SUIT) AND BOB PERFORMING IN HIGH SCHOOL **RIGHT** THEIR SENIOR PICTURES, WEARING WHAT THEY WORE TO PROM **PREVIOUS PAGES** DAVID AND BOB FINALLY TOGETHER AT A COLLEGE FORMAL

BOB It had stewed for such a long time that when it happened it was hot in every way.

all over again. So there was always something going on. But David and I had become such important figures to one another—it was almost like there was a time when it was the right thing to do rather than just tawdry.

DAVID Oh, I had lots of boyfriends before Bob. I can't say I was a slut, but you know, pubescent slap and tickle. I didn't go there with Bob, because I didn't think he would respect me if he thought I was a tramp. So I just played it cool until I was sure.

I think I really knew the summer after graduating high school. He was going to go to Notre Dame, and his parents wanted him to. But I talked him out of it. And that's when I thought . . .

BOB He really didn't have to talk me out of it. I didn't want to be away from him. And I didn't want to go back to a whole Catholic regimen at a university that did noth-

ing for me. Then you stacked that up against going to Kent State, a very liberal school with someone you're mad about.

We lived in separate dorm rooms that first year of college, but we always had dinner together. It was really a natural progression that had stewed for such a long time that when it finally happened it was hot in every way—mentally, physically. It was just really wonderful.

Sophomore year we moved out of the dorm and lived together. That was the first time we had a situation where we weren't trying to sneak it in somewhere. And actually, we shared the apartment with two other guys, so we had to be somewhat discreet.

At that time, the general campus community did not support homosexuality. Even at our school, a hotbed of anti-Vietnam War activities, the Gay Liberation Front was on the fringe. So everybody was still, on the whole, very discreet.

Ironically, since homosexuality is being discussed, that was the one thing that you could use to get out of the draft, but it was so shameful that I don't think either one of us would have employed it. If we were drafted, we would have gone to Canada or something. But it wouldn't have occurred to us to use sexuality, because that was just such a . . . such a non-alternative.

DAVID People didn't flaunt their gayness around town or around school. And I still remember the first time I went to a gay bar. It's such a cliché, but I thought, Oh my God, there's more of us. And, you know, the way you got outed was that you'd go to the gay bar and see this one and that one.

But some people were out. It was all that post-Stonewall euphoria. There was a gay organization on campus and there was sort of this burgeoning of gay-related stuff. Like on television, *Mary Tyler Moore* had a gay theme on one episode. And then there were shows like *Soap*: Billy Crystal had this character and he was gay; it really was kind of a big deal at the time.

That was also the first sort of flowering of the disco phase and the whole bathhouse fuck-fest. We could have participated in that unbridled sex thing but, because I was in a relationship, I was not interested in doing that. Thank goodness.

I recognized really early that something was up. Before we moved to New York for good, I would come to do internships—and this was '81 and '82. By '82, there were those little rumors about the gay cancer. And we have had a lot of friends die of AIDS. Luckily, none of our really close friends.

BOB We were so young when we moved to New York. We went out two or three nights a week to party—and on the weekend. So we had a helluva good time. And we always had the security that no matter how fucked up things got anywhere else, we had one another. We also had wonderful careers going; we were the upwardly mobile, nothing's-gonna-stop-us duo.

Everything gets put into perspective when something goes wrong. In 2000, David had congestive heart failure. Going through that changed my perspective on absolutely everything. Because I'm in the room with somebody I love and they're saying, "If we can't catch him now, he's going to die." And we never thought that would happen in our forties; we thought we would be together until we were in our eighties. That was a big deal. You know, prom night was like pushing the elevator button by comparison.

When my mother found out, she said, "You have to have him not work, you must take care of him and you must do everything you can to make his life flawlessly easy." And it was at that point that she really fully acknowledged that what we have is beyond something casual. And, you know, she was saying, "Anything you can do, you have to do. No matter what." And, of course, I already was.

"We've all ended up being happy ever after," says Bob, who never officially came out to his family. "In the beginning, we wouldn't do that, out of not wanting to hurt them or cause them shame, and probably because of fear of rejection. The nice thing about the fact that we've been together for such a long time is that we've all grown comfortable with this."

"But they know the story; they're not fools," adds David, who has recovered from his health scare. "I just never felt like I needed their validation or approval."

As they celebrate more than thirty years as a couple (and almost thirty-five as best friends), Bob notes that when he and David were growing up, "we never thought there would be such a thing as 'gay rights.' Looking at it from the eighth-grade point-of-view, I was gonna be happy if I wasn't getting beaten up everyday. So, in that respect, life is a million times better than I ever really thought it would be."

THE
REBEL

AVRAM FINKELSTEIN

WESTBURY HIGH SCHOOL
LONG ISLAND, NEW YORK
CLASS OF **1969**

"I campaigned for John F. Kennedy. I must have been eight-years-old and I was obsessed. In hindsight, I guess you could make the argument that I thought he was cute," says Avram Finkelstein, who was one of the first in the gay community to ACT UP.

"I was a red-diaper baby. That's what kids of lefties are called. My parents met at a lefty summer camp; my father worked with Ethel Rosenberg; my grandmother used to come to peace marches with me. So I was raised in one of those households where it would have been more abnormal to *not* be politically engaged," explains Avram, who applied tactics learned during his activist youth to fighting AIDS and, most specifically, to the design and distribution of the landmark Silence = Death poster.

It's not surprising that, amidst the riots, sex and drugs of the summer of 1969, prom was not on the top of Avram's to-do list. In fact, he was out of town that night, protesting the Vietnam War in Boston.

THERE ARE TWO TYPES OF KIDS: the type who wants to fit in and the type that doesn't want to. And some people make an identity out of not fitting in, because they either have no option or they like that. Here I have a name Avram Finkelstein; I mean, there's no way I could fit in.

To make matters even more extreme, my brother, who is two years older, had problems with his eyes, so he was a slow learner and was bussed to an all-black school, because they didn't have special-ed in the school I was at. That tainted him. And he preceded me by a year in school. And I think people had already made an assessment of me in the same way that, if your brother is an athlete, you become popular. Aside from being "Finkelstein's brother," I think I carved my own niche of being an outcast by being shy and being a vegan and by being probably a little overly artistic.

"I'm totally flummoxed by people who have any nostalgia for their high school days."

I didn't have a lot of friends. And the friends that I did have were mainly made through family contact with other lefty kids. Most of them were older, so they weren't in high school with me. A lot of them lived in New York City, and I used to go there all the time, especially the summer before I went into high school. I would go to concerts and hang out with my hippie friends and we would panhandle and buy food and just hang out in Central Park. So, my world was very different from the world in high school. In that world, I had to make do and get along.

On prom night I was probably stoned off my ass, sleeping on the floor in Boston. Not that if I had stayed, I would have gone.

I'm totally flummoxed by people who have any nostalgia for their high school days. I hated everything about it and I never felt part of that community for many reasons. So I can't imagine why I would have gone to the prom. In fact, one reason I didn't go is that I had moved up to Boston before I even graduated.

I moved to get away and find an apartment, but it was also the height of the student strikes. The Museum School in Boston, which is where I ended up going to college, was producing posters that all the other colleges would come pick up and wheat paste around town. The school was open twenty-four hours, and people were sleeping there, and there were stacks of posters drying in the hallway. And I was going up there to do that for the summer.

So on prom night I was probably stoned off my ass, sleeping on the floor in Boston. Not that if I had stayed on Long Island I would have gone to prom. I think I went to one dance; it was in junior high school, and I blanked it out it was so uncomfortable.

Now, there's another part of the story that I think is worth mentioning. Which is that it was the '60s. A lot of people thought it was uncool to go to the prom, and my friends in particular thought it was very uncool. A few of them did go, but they got high and goofed on it. If you went to the prom, you were "straight," in the old sense. You were a goody-goody. You were a cheerleader. You were an overachiever. And my friends were anything but that.

The fact that it wasn't cool gave me a reason to feel comfortable about not going. But the reason I didn't go was that I didn't feel safe, because I was gay. I was tormented for being gay by that com-munity. I mean, I was one of those sissy boys who couldn't walk home from school without having a gang of kids chasing me.

But actually, I probably could have gone without getting the shit kicked out of me. At that point, I started dealing drugs in high school to pay for my own drugs. When all the straight kids who used to beat the crap out of me found out that I was into drugs, all of a sudden they were my best friends. But I didn't want anything to do with them and I didn't want to celebrate my history with that community, because I felt they were total fucks. They made my life completely miserable, and I was obstinate enough to not want to forgive them for it.

One thought that's occurred to me is, What would it have been like to have had to make a decision about prom after *Will & Grace*? Because being out in high school was inconceivable. It might as well have been 1952. Leo Kutch was my closest friend, and people knew he was a fag: he was one of those queens who was so out that there was never going to be a debate. But I don't think that he ever had an easy time of it. And all the indications about being gay in my house were that it wasn't okay. That was the line in the sand—I could support the Weather Underground all I wanted, but I couldn't be gay. So, I didn't come out until I was in college. I did the classic gay thing of leaving town to reinvent myself.

Stonewall happened that June after prom. I remember reading about it in the *Village Voice* and not necessarily seeing it as significant. You have to bear in mind, it was the early days of the gay rights movement and, in a way, gay rights hadn't become a thing yet. Still, Leo thought Stonewall was big news, but I didn't make the connection. I think I was too self-oppressed to make that connection. To see it as a great thing.

That summer I got a job working for the city of Boston with my friend Alan in an educational program in one of the poorer neighborhoods; it was very hippie—we had a van, like an old

milk truck, full of art supplies and we would go from place to place every day and have some sort of communal workshop. And Alan— god, what was his last name?—he had dreadlocks; he was the most beautiful black boy. So I ended up falling madly in love with him. That was a really seminal thing for me: I don't think I really felt like it was okay to be gay until I felt loved—until I had a relationship that was ongoing, that wasn't just about sex.

But the love of my life, the thing that stopped the presses, was when I met Don, which was in 1978. That was it; I was looking no further. He came from a large Italian family, all musicians except the mother; and I was there all the time.

Don was the first person I knew with AIDS. My mother was a doctor of sciences—biochemistry and microbiology—and she diagnosed that there was something wrong with his immune system before AIDS was even a word. The first time I introduced them, he came home with me and he struck a fever that night. So, you can't have a boyfriend strike a fever in the middle of the night with a Jewish mother who's also a bio-chemist and not have her notice.

At the time Don was beginning to get sick, it was called GRID— Gay-Related Immune Deficiency. He had a sinus infection that wouldn't go away; he'd be in and out of doctors' offices for very small things that just would never go away, but wouldn't be diagnosed. I was reading about GRID, you know, in various newspapers and in the *New York Native*. And I was making the connection, via my mother's suggestion, that there was something wrong with his immune system.

I started to be fearful that that's what was going on. And it was.

He progressively got sicker and sicker. Before that, his family was very accepting of him and very accepting of me—I was a member of the family. But the day after the funeral, they came to my apartment and took everything. Everything that was his and everything that they thought was his. Sweaters that were mine that he wore, because he would get cold all the time. Everything. I realized that they actually thought I had absolutely had no right to his life, and that I was only there for a little while. Of course, the subtext to AIDS in that case is that if I'm not directly to blame for infecting their son, I'm indirectly to blame for representing the act or the "lifestyle" that led to their son being sick in the first place.

Now, if we were married—if we were a straight couple—they never would have come into my house and taken things out of the closet; it would have been under-stood. I can't tell you how many times I wasn't allowed in to visit Don. And what is the whole marriage debate about if it's not about rights to get into a hospital room? I think marriage is bullshit, but I understand why gay activists are obsessed with it. Politi-cally and economically I don't think it's bullshit; I think it's significant.

And I think going to the prom is, in hind-sight, very significant. The prom signifies a way in which gay people have to adapt to the greater world surrounding them, because there's the heterosexual matchmaking subtext.

No one was dealing with AIDS. Because, you know, gays were disposable. But Rock Hudson was a tragedy.

SILENCE=DEATH

SILENCE=DE

sted at an **AIDS Rally in Manhattan**

tors holding hands during a moment of silence yes- | outside the United States Court House. P
oley Square. A march and rally sponsored by the | testers for disorderly conduct. They

Gays protest lack of d to wage war against A

By FRANCES McMORRIS
Daily News Staff Writer

Seventeen demonstrator disorderly conduct yesterd which nearly 200 chanting, ers blocked morning rush-h nancial District to protest availability of anti-AIDS dr

The protesters gathered on Broadway near Wall St. between 7 and 9:30 a.m. and burned an effigy of federal Food and Drug Administrator Frank Young.

Sixteen men and one woman were taken away by stretcher and placed in police paddy wagons after "they sat down in the middle of the street," said police spokeswoman Janice Swinney. They were later given summonses for disorderly conduct.

"We're basically protesting the fact that the government is sitting on eight drugs that are more promising ... than AZT," said Larry Kramer, organizer of the rally and co-founder of the Gay Men's Health Crisis.

Fury and rage

"The point really is the growing fury and rage in the affected communities that nothing is being done and no

TOP RIGHT AND LEFT AVRAM IN THE PRESS DURING EARLY ACT UP DEMONSTRATIONS **ABOVE RIGHT AND LEFT** GRAPHICS CREATED WITH THE SILENCE = DEATH PROJECT, LATER RENAMED GRAN FURY

Times/Sara Krulwich

ested 32 pro-manding in-

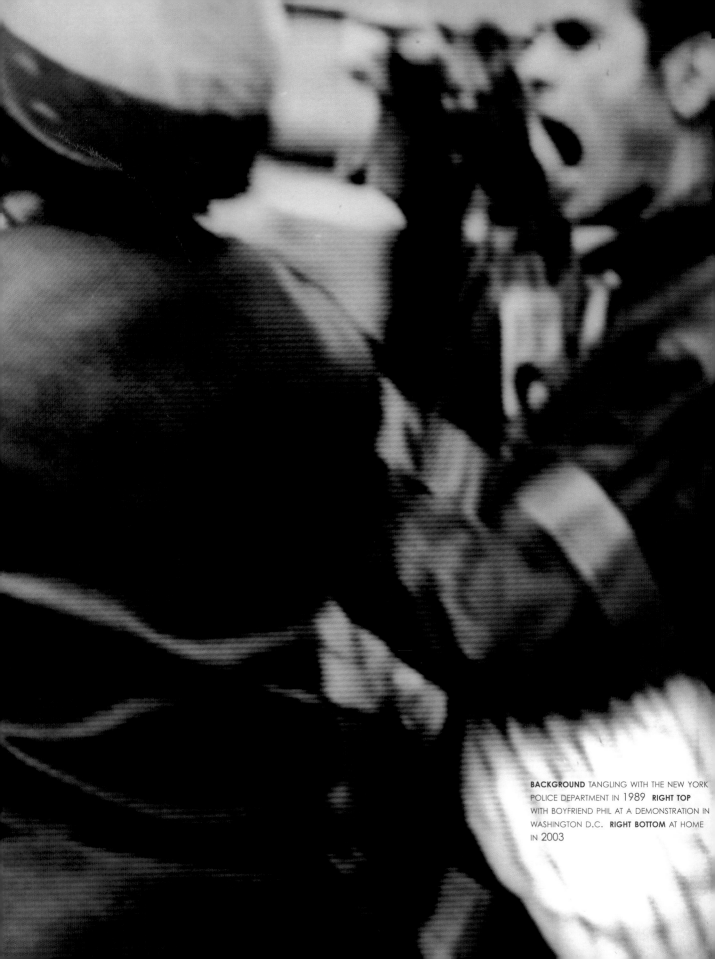

BACKGROUND TANGLING WITH THE NEW YORK
POLICE DEPARTMENT IN 1989 **RIGHT TOP**
WITH BOYFRIEND PHIL AT A DEMONSTRATION IN
WASHINGTON D.C. **RIGHT BOTTOM** AT HOME
IN 2003

What it says when you can't bring a same-sex date to the prom is that you're destructive to the community just by being yourself. Which is the gay rights struggle.

This is seminal to my politic: there's always a dividing line. With straight people, there's always a dividing line and you never know when you're going to hit up against it. No matter how progressive a community, a person or a family member thinks they are, there is a dividing line past which they have no idea what our lives are about and they have no idea what constitutes acceptance from our point of view.

Getting involved in AIDS activism—of course, it was about Don's death. But the turning point was about a year later when Rock Hudson died. I remember thinking, This is the most horrible thing in the world. That the world should care that Rock Hudson—a total stranger that people think they knew because he was on the screen, but who was a horrible role model because he was such a closet case—that the world should care that he died and no one should know that Don died was a terrible, terrible thing. It threw me into a tailspin and made me realize that there were little deaths that were just as big and that *that's* what needed to be said. No one was dealing with AIDS, because it didn't really matter. Because, you know, gays were disposable. Or the black community was, you know, disposable. But Rock Hudson was a tragedy.

This was in 1985. I was having dinner with two friends one night, and we were talking about how there was really no place to talk about being a gay man in the age of AIDS. We decided we were going to form a small group based on the consciousness-raising model from the feminist movement—which was to have a potluck every week at a different person's house. We each invited one person, and those six people started meeting.

Every time we would start talking about AIDS, we would end up talking about politics. It became obvious that there was a political question that wasn't being addressed. I knew we couldn't be the only people thinking this, but there was no context in which to have the discussion. Now, it had been my experience in the '60s that when people needed to communicate to one another outside of the mainstream press, they did it on the street via graffiti and posters. So I thought, Why not try this? It's time honored; maybe it will work. And I said to the group, "What about if we were to do a poster about it?"

POSTSCRIPT

They finished up the poster in December of '86. "We decided to put it up in the spring, because there aren't as many people out on the streets in winter." Three weeks later, ACT UP began.

Then-boyfriend Simon Doonan encouraged Avram to bring his poster to one of the first demonstrations. Subsequently, "Silence = Death" became the rallying cry for the protesters who, through a series of radical, media-savvy actions, sent a message that AIDS activists were angry, organized and a force to be reckoned with.

It's still a potent icon. "On one hand, I'm like, 'We obviously did something that withstood the test of time.' But anything from back then that still seems pertinent brings up the disturbing notion that very little has changed."

Avram believes the days of AIDS protests are effectively over, because "you cannot revisit that same topic with any vivacity and expect any change." But he still considers himself radical. "I've noticed there's a rhythm with me, that every seven or eight years I'll have a real burst of overt political activity," explains the displaced Manhattanite, now living in upstate New York with his partner Phil, whom he met in ACT UP.

"I'm actually very shy," says Avram, who started GroovyQ, a T-shirt and accessories company, with Phil and a friend. "So I would not customarily go to meetings unless it was really dire. And I think it is." While not sure when and how he'll get involved, he's not worried: "One of the things you learn as a Jew is constant vigilance. I'll be really scared if I sleep through it." That's what concerns him about the queer community's current trajectory. "*Will & Grace* is a great thing for the kid that thinks he can take his boyfriend to the prom. But it's bad if you grow up thinking everything's okay. Because when you find out it isn't, it may be too late."

THE
ACCIDENTAL
ACTIVIST

DANNY GARVIN

RICE HIGH SCHOOL
NEW YORK, NEW YORK
CLASS OF **1966**

Stonewall was a defining moment for gay history, but not for Danny. "When history is being made, you don't necessarily know it," he notes. "I was just your average gay kid coming out and dealing with it."

There were, however, a series of events preceding Stonewall that brought the nineteen-year-old to the Village the night the rioting began. His mother passed away and his father moved to Ireland; Danny was given the option of finishing up school in Ireland or enlisting. He joined the Navy, where he graduated with a high-school equivalency degree, but without a prom. "I thought I'd see the world, but I ended up being stationed in Brooklyn."

After an unplanned gay encounter—and one sought— while on leave, "I discovered that if I stood across from the base hitchhiking, I'd always meet a guy in a car. So that's basically how I started. I was still dating women at the time. I told myself it was a phase." Danny eventually realized it wasn't, and had a breakdown.

He committed himself, but never disclosed his gay tendencies, fearing he would be dishonorably discharged. The Navy, faced with the prospect of paying the teen's medical bills for life, offered him a deal: they would discharge him with honor if he "acknowledged" his psychological problems started before signing up, thereby forfeiting any veterans' benefits. Danny agreed.

I TURNED EIGHTEEN on March 1 and I got out of the Navy on March 17—St. Patrick's Day. I came home and stayed with my sister, who took over my father's apartment when he moved to Ireland.

One night I went down to the Village to Julius' (that's the bar at the beginning of the movie, *Boys in the Band*). And this older guy said, "What are you doing here? You should be around the corner with all the chicken at that bar that just opened." So I walked over to the Stonewall and saw all these guys dancing. And I said to myself, This'll never last. So I was at Stonewall on opening night.

> "I walked over to the Stonewall and saw all these guys dancing. And I said to myself, This'll never last."

That was 1967, at the height of the hippie movement. There was a whole sexual revolution going on. I would go through periods; I didn't go out with women for a while, then I got hooked up with this prostitute Rusty. We went out for five, six months, then she started going out with this guy who I had been to bed with. You know, it was a different time period. There were not so many labels: we were all experimenting with our sexuality; we were all starting to find out who we were.

By 1969, there was a break going on within the gay move—well, it wasn't a "movement," but within gay society. There were guys that went to the hairstylist and wore the mod clothes, and then there was the other group of us that would smoke pot and try LSD and protest against the war. I mean, I had a boyfriend freak out on me

> There's the part of me that wants to say, "Yes, I picked up a brick. I threw it at the cop." In reality, I was running like other people.

because I wore a bell around my neck. He was like, "What are you doing wearing that thing?" Because it represented hippies.

At the time, I was living in a gay commune on Bleecker Street. It was three rooms, and there were basically nine of us who lived there. You slept wherever you got to sleep; tricks were there; food was for everybody; and there was no pressure to pay rent or anything.

Even though the Stonewall was getting a little tired by June of '69, it was the largest gay bar in the city and the only place to dance in the Village. That's why I was going there that night with my friend Keith Murdock, who was home from college. We walked up from Bleecker Street on Seventh Avenue, then over to Christopher. And we saw people being pulled out, you know?

Of course there's the part of me that just wants to say, "Oh, yes, I picked up a brick. I threw it at the cop," and "Oh, yeah, they hit me with clubs." In reality, I was running like a bunch of other people when a cop came at me with a nightstick. I was

back there screaming and taunting, making the catcalls. Did I pick up the brick? No. But I still wouldn't today because, you know, when those bricks got thrown, it wasn't always a cop that got hit. And when the Molotov cocktails were lit and thrown, it wasn't always hitting the target. It is dramatic, but you may hit a car and set it off. Or some innocent bystander. And then there are other people who would say, "Yes, but that is the cost of revolution."

On the second night, people were down there; word of mouth had got around that this had happened. Usually when there's a police raid on a bar it would be closed maybe one night, two tops. But this was different—a riot had taken place. So people went down there and, you know, "We want our bar back . . . We're gonna take it back." So people were smashing open the doors. The police sent rein-forcements, because there were people attacking property. Of course, people have now had more time to think, Well, if I had been here the night before, this is what I would have done.

Also, whenever there was a raid before, in a bar or something like that, people would panic. I mean, actual panic. You know? You talk about

Raid Stirs Melee

the Stone-   with the disturbances, whi
frequented   continued for more than t o
5.   hours. By the a
ast o   urned to d an

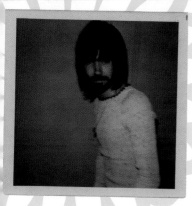

losing your life, your career, your family. There was no, "Let's fight together"; there was no sense of, "This is ours, we have rights." The thing that came about with Stonewall was, all of a sudden, there was, "Wait, this is *our* bar."

But if it was another gay bar that had gotten raided, like Keller's the leather bar, it wouldn't have had that impact. Because the people would have been older. Like the Mattachine Society: these were "old" guys—in their thirties—who believed that we should change the laws from within. I can remember after the Stonewall riots, like a few days later, they were handing out pamphlets saying, "This is not the way to go. These riots are not the way to go." But it's different when you raid a bar where there are young kids who've been away at college campuses, kids that have been in demonstrations and already have the knowledge of civil disobedience. It was already, "We're not taking your society." That was the way my generation thought of things back then.

Because it was not just Stonewall; the whole country was changing. Just go back ten short years to '59: there was no Pill, if you had sex without a condom you got pregnant . . . black people were not allowed to vote in certain states. With my generation, we heard women saying, "I don't want to wear bras anymore." All of a sudden people were saying, "I'm not colored. I'm Negro." I mean, before Stonewall, you had your gay coffee shops, you had gay bars and clothes stores, but the only way you found out was that someone brought you there. The difference after Stonewall was: it became, for a little while there, more in your face, more confrontational.

We discovered a power that we didn't know we had. And the Gay Activists Alliance and the Gay Liberation Front came about because of the riots.

So, where does prom fit in?

It was a few years later. I was twenty-one and working in a gay bar called the Zoo; it was the first in New York to have a back-room. I was living in the East Village with George, a Jesuit priest, and Morty Manford. Morty's parents were the ones who founded PFLAG. (That was the first time that I had known or seen anybody's family so support-ive of their child being gay.)

But what happened was George decided he was going to move down to Florida. My father had just moved back; he couldn't take living in Ireland. But he couldn't get an apartment because he was over sixty-five, and in New York City there are rules that if you're over sixty-five and you get into a rent stabilized apartment they cannot raise your rent; so no one wanted to rent to him. I was able to get the apartment in my name and I moved in with him. My father wouldn't go to the East Village, so we moved back uptown.

I didn't call her or see her after prom night. But she called me ten years later.

I was back in my old neighborhood and I was seeing my old friends. We were no longer teenagers going off and having gang fights. So I thought, Okay, maybe it's time to change. Even during the riots, I probably thought I'd get married and settle down. I knew gay guys who all of a sudden got engaged. And I think, again, that had to do with there being no real support system for gay kids. You came out and you had one place to go: gay bars. I remember being in Julius', standing with my back to the bar, and being tapped on the shoulder and asked to turn around because they could be closed for soliciting. This life did not offer you safety, even at a gay bar there was no safety. Who wants that? Any normal person would say, "No, I don't want that." Not if I can go out and laugh and dance and not worry about being arrested or being beaten up. Yes, there were the early days of, "Yeah this is great. We did this whole revolution." But no one had any idea where it was gonna go; we'd never had a positive gay future.

At the time, my best friend Dougie was going out with this girl Josie. She was best friends with this girl Maryanne. I met them at a bar one night. And Maryanne liked me. She was maybe seventeen, eighteen. The age difference was acceptable then; a lot of girls were getting married at eighteen. But I knew it wasn't going to go anywhere. It was more a question on my own of, "Am I this way or am I that way? Let's find out."

We had had one or two dates together. And we're having drinks one night, and Josie says Maryanne wants to ask me to the prom. I never had the chance to have that experience. And when I was a kid, prom night was like the big thing in the neighborhood. The girls would come down in their gowns, the guys would be in their tuxes, their first tux. People'd be lining up on the stoops and taking pictures. This was like the rite of passage into adulthood. So to be asked to one, it was like, "Oh this is great!" So I said, "Alright."

We went to a prom dinner at the school. They had it in the gym; actually it was an all-girls Catholic school, so maybe it was in the cafeteria. Of course, we all had to say grace before the meal. There was no King or Queen that I remember. But I can remember everybody wanting to basically get away from those nuns and go drinking.

The gowns were all long then. But I remember my tux better than her gown: it had this big bow tie, like I was being attacked by a bat. I also remember we rented a limo for the night, you know, so that we were able to drink in it.

The prom ended at ten o'clock and then we went down to the Copa, and it was all prom kids in there. Then, of course, you'd do the ferry thing; it was a thing in the neighborhood to take a ride on the Staten Island Ferry at the end of the prom night 'cause it's romantic. And then I brought her home.

I gave her a kiss good night. I didn't try to cop any tit or anything. I knew she was a virgin, so if I did cop a feel, she might have been, "What are you doing?" and it could have turned into a bad experience. And, of course, there's the underlying thing of, What if she does respond? Then there's the responsibility of taking her virginity. And that leads deeper into a relationship.

I didn't call her or see her or anything after prom night. But she called me ten years later. I had already come out and had been living in California for two years with this guy; we had been together like eight years. We broke up and I came back to New York. And all of a sudden my phone rang one night—it was Maryanne.

And I said, "Oh my God, how are you?" So she said, "Oh, fine." Then she asked, "Are you married?" (I guess she couldn't figure out I was gay; I had a hard enough time figuring it out.) So I said, "No, I'm not married." Even though I had come out, had a lover, all my friends were gay and I had accepted myself as being gay, all of a sudden it was like *boom*: I'm hit with this fear from the past, like when I would run into somebody from the neighborhood, and it was like, Okay, let's open the closet door and get inside.

So Maryanne's talking and saying that she had gotten married. "I married this guy, and he looked just like you!" So I said, "Oh . . ." And she goes, "I really fell for you back then, I loved you. I think I even married him because he looked like you . . . You know, when we were back at the prom, I would have let you taken my virginity that night. I really thought you would have been the first guy. I really, really fell for you."

LEFT TOP IN THE '80S IN THE WEST VILLAGE **FAR LEFT** DANNY AT THE 1987 MARCH ON WASHINGTON WITH FRIENDS **ABOVE** CELEBRATING STONEWALL'S TWENTY-FIFTH ANNIVERSARY WITH OTHER VETERANS OF THE RIOTS

POSTSCRIPT

This was the opening Danny needed; "I didn't realize that," he responded, "but I was dealing with being gay." Not to be deterred, Maryanne pushed for the chance to convert him, but Danny declined. "She called me once after that, drunk. And that was it." Danny heard from his sister that Maryanne passed away a few years later. "Maybe the last phone call back to me was her trying to reach back to a happier time in her life," he wonders aloud. "The prom was a happy time for her."

As for Danny, who's been with his partner Rick for eleven years, he seems pretty happy these days albeit self-conscious that he's becoming too conservative: "I'm living in a building with a doorman. I work for Columbia University. I wear a suit and a tie. The whole thing. Is there a part of me that says, 'Oh, let me talk to you about when I was doing drugs in the Stonewall?' Yes. But that was a different life, a different person."

Like it or not, he'll probably be talking about Stonewall forever. "I get dusted off every June," he jokes. "It's very odd; I was just going out to dance that night. I never thought that I'd become one of the people talking about it"— especially given the fact that his experience contradicts gay lore that it was a horde of drag queens that sparked the revolution.

"Watch the news after any gay pride parade: they always show drag queens. You'd think it was a parade of all drag queens; it's the same with Stonewall," he explains. "And I always feel that that's the story people want to hear."

THE GAY
MOM

MARGARET MANSON

CAMELBACK HIGH SCHOOL
PHOENIX, ARIZONA
CLASS OF **1961**

Her father was killed in a car accident when she was eleven, leaving her mother to raise four kids. A few years later, Margaret—smart, but rebellious—was sent to live with her stepsister. "I left California mid-semester of my junior year and went to Phoenix with the idea that I was going to start over again."

Unfortunately, her new home proved unstable and her stepsister abusive. "There was a point where I literally had no shoes, and I'm in a high school where appearance is really important," she remembers.

She was lonely and sad, but not unpopular. "Because I was a pretty, little blond, I always had boyfriends," says Margaret, who attended several proms and married at twenty. "In Phoenix, I had a boyfriend who was the Homecoming King and a football star."

She also had close girl-friends. "But I didn't even have a context for understanding anything about sexuality, much less the idea of being sexually attracted to girls," explains the mother of three, who followed her middle son's lead, coming out just a few years after he did.

THE FIRST PROM I WENT TO was probably when I was a freshman in California. And I went with a kid who was a junior. It was a really big deal to be a freshman and be asked out by a junior or a senior to go to their prom.

I remember that we wore these massive dresses with big skirts, very long. The proms in those days—you didn't have a stretch limousine, and so you would go in a car and you'd go out to dinner. Then you'd go to the dance, which was in the school gymnasium and highly chaperoned. You might be able to stay out until midnight, but the idea of going to a party afterwards, I mean, I'd never even heard of any of that. So it was certainly a very different prom experience than my kids had twenty years later.

> "You might be able to stay out until midnight, but the idea of going to a party afterwards . . . I'd never even heard of that. So it was certainly a very different prom experience than my kids had twenty years later."

My senior prom would have been in Arizona. I remember our Senior Getaway Day, but I don't remember the senior prom, and it may have been that I didn't go. At that point, my high school experience was pretty unhappy. And it probably wasn't something that I would have been able to do in terms of having a dress and being able to do all that. Ultimately there were so many things going on with me in Arizona that I just didn't do well there. And I think they finally graduated me because they didn't know what to do with me.

Jim and I both knew from the time Steven was little that he was probably gay, but we never spoke the word.

I came back to California and decided to sort of redefine myself again. I started at El Camino College, but by the second semester I was not particularly interested in studying. So I dropped out and moved to Los Angeles. I got a job at the telephone company selling princess phones; you know, I used to try to talk people into buying different colors to match the decor in each room.

I remember one morning going to work, looking around the office, and sort of having this epiphany: I literally had no skills and so this would be my job—this would be it. So I quit and went home and went back to school and had to get As and Bs to be able to get an associate's degree to transfer. That was a turning point in my life.

I met Jim when I was nineteen; he was twenty-six. I turned twenty and we literally got married two weeks later. I was just finishing up at El Camino, and so I married him and then I went on to Cal State-Long Beach and finished my bachelor's degree in English.

The first time I found myself really attracted to a woman was in 1966. I had heard that the Catholic schools would hire you if you had a bachelor's degree and you didn't have a teaching credential. So not being Catholic, I looked in the phonebook under "Saint" and I sent off thirteen letters to all the "Saint" schools. Nine of them wanted to interview me, and I was hired by one to teach second grade. I had fifty-five eight-year-olds, and I had never taught in my whole entire life. But I was twenty-two; it never occurred to me I couldn't do it.

Sister Ann Peter—Penny—taught the other second-grade class. And we became very good friends. She was the first woman that I really fell deeply in love with. And there was a time in here where I left my marriage; and Penny and I lived together for a little while.

I was so deeply attracted to this woman—but it never really occurred to me that women wouldn't be attracted to women. But it

was probably pretty frightening; I really did not know what to do with it. And I left that relationship and I went back to my marriage. Soon after that I had my first son, Matthew.

Steven was born in 1972. And Jim and I both knew from the time Steven was little that he was probably gay. But, as hard as it is to believe, Jim and I never spoke of it together; we never spoke the word.

Here's my disclaimer: Jim is a really fine man and he was a good father, but he is the oldest son of the oldest son of a Greek immigrant. So, one of the reasons why I didn't talk about it—and I'm not proud of this—is that Jim was so homophobic. And there was so much negativity about homosexuals that I kept the peace in the family by not raising the issue.

And yet I knew. When Steven was probably in about the second grade, one of his teachers wrote in his report card, "There is one thing I'm concerned about: the fact that he only plays with girls. And if this continues next year, you should really be concerned." And I challenged her and I was very angry with her for even suggesting that Steven might not be masculine. And I dismissed it, but in my heart of hearts I knew what she was talking about.

But, you know, what do we do with it? First of all, you don't even have the word "gay" at that point—you have "homosexual." And you have "the homosexuals who molest the little kids in the bathroom," and you have this perversion out there in the '70s where there's something really wrong about this lifestyle and about this child. But Steven was a wonderful kid and very popular. And I always was very protective and I was always very close with him. I think that for me it was: I didn't know what to do with it.

And I keep saying that, but there were no options. It was all about "Who's your son dating?" and "Who's he taking to the prom?" And so you create these illusions of heterosexuality to protect yourself as the parent. And, you know, raising children is pretty much an ego trip in a lot of ways. So you have these kids who perform well in school, they're very popular and people would always say to me, "Well, does Steven have a girlfriend?" And my response would be, "Well, yeah, he has this girlfriend" or "No, he doesn't, but he has these really close friends."

Steven was never, ever, ever romantically interested in girls. Ever. He took a girl to the prom

CLOCKWISE FROM ABOVE IN 1969;
PROM 1958; PROM 1959; IN 1965;
HIGH SCHOOL GRADUATION 1962
PREVIOUS PAGES AT 1958 PROM;
AND IN HER EARLY TEENS

who was—he was voted most likely to succeed and so was she. And they went as friends. I think that in some ways, it was almost like a validation to the exterior world, "Well, look my son's going to the prom." Even though I knew, without articulating it, that she wasn't a girlfriend, I don't think I was ready to acknowledge it.

And I had clues all the way along. After his junior year in high school, he went off to Boys State in Sacramento. He met a kid there and came back, and there was some communication he had with this boy. He may have been at the point of maybe wanting to talk about it, but I could never bring myself to have that conversation with him.

A few years later, Steven had been at Berkeley for a couple of years, and we're at the beach—we had a house at Capistrano Beach every summer—and we're walking on the sand, and Steven is telling me about some of his friends at Berkeley. And I can't remember exactly how he's talking about it, but somehow he tells me they're gay. And I remember saying to him, "Is this a lifestyle you've chosen for yourself?" And Steven said, "It's not a choice." And he said to me, "I haven't told dad, but I will." So that night I went to bed, and in the middle of

> # I realized that, even if it wasn't Sandy, my life needed to go in a different direction than my marriage.

the night I woke up and I was crying. Jim asked, "What's wrong?" And I told him. And he said to me, "I knew this day would come."

At that point, we had an exchange student from France. She was in San Diego, and I had to pick her up; so Steven and I got in the car in San Juan Capistrano and we drove to San Diego together. And I'm driving down the 405 and I'm sobbing and I'm telling Steven—this is the very next day after he told me—and I told him, I said, "Steven, there are many ways in this world to be happy. And this is the way you're going to live your life. And it's going to be okay. And here's my promise to you: We're a package deal. If there's any-

one out there who rejects you, they've rejected me. And I don't care who that is." And I can tell you—with that strong will and determination that got me in trouble and out of trouble throughout my life—I meant it. I absolutely meant it.

When we got back home, I got my mom and stepdad on the phone, and I said, "I wanna

tell you this right now; I don't want to have to repeat it. We have been given a rare gift. We have been given an opportunity to love and know Steven as the person he really is." And I said, "That takes great courage and dignity on his part. And we are not gonna let this boy down." And his father, by the way, did the right thing also. He rose to meet the occasion and has never, ever, ever rejected his son.

I think, in some sort of weird way, Steven gave me the courage to examine my own life. Jim and I had been much better parents than we had been partners. And in 1993, I was still married—but I met Sandy. And from the first time I met her, I was just absolutely drawn to her. I

LEFT WITH JIM AND THEIR THREE SONS IN 1980 **ABOVE** WITH SANDY AND THE BOYS IN 2003
BELOW WITH SANDY AT STEVEN AND ERIK'S COMMITMENT CEREMONY

was a college administrator at the time and she's a social worker, and we were working on a coalition together. And we wrote a grant together; it was not funded, but we continued to see each other through this coalition. And somewhere in all of this I realized that, even if it wasn't Sandy out there as part of my future, that my life needed to go in a different direction than my marriage.

And, as I said earlier, I believed that being attracted to a woman was—that basically every woman felt the way I did. Then I did a little survey with some of my very dearest friends, who I knew would tell me the truth. And they all said to me, "Sorry to tell you this: we're not." I kinda had to come to terms with that, too.

At that point I was the director of human resources for the college, in a highly visible position. And as I took stock of my life, I said to myself, "Margaret, you've done everything society has expected you to: you were educated, you were married, you've raised three wonderful children, they're educated. You've done everything right." And I said, "I don't feel that there's anything anyone has any right to ask of me. So now I'm gonna live my life. And people can accept or reject me, but that'll be their choice." That was my guiding principle.

So, that was kind of how all that happened. I talked to the kids about Sandy. And all of those boys, independent of each other, said, "You've given a great deal to others; it's about time for you to be happy." So, I honestly figured: if my kids are okay, who else matters? Do I really care what the chancellor's secretary thinks?

"Sandy and I have been together since 1995. And it is the clearest, purest relationship I've ever had," says Margaret. "I married my husband because I loved him; it didn't feel at all fraudulent at the time. But my relationship with Sandy is the most uncomplicated and the most uncompromised that I've had."

Of course, her relationship with her son Steven has become less complicated, too. "There's a comfort level there, certainly with Steven and his partner Erik, that Sandy and I have. We have a different understanding of one aspect of life that I don't have with others, but beyond that, I'm really close with all of the boys."

And even though she feels she didn't do enough to make her son's coming out easier, it's hard to argue with the results: Steven is kind, smart and successful. And in 2002, he and Erik celebrated their commitment with a ceremony in Provincetown that included Margaret, Sandy, Jim and Margaret's parents.

"We love Erik, and I really feel like they're soul mates," says Margaret. "They have this wonderful relationship. And it was publicly recognized by family and friends. And that was very powerful."

"They'll probably have the first grandchildren," she adds. "You never know."

SENIORS

The Depression pushed kids out of jobs, into high schools. There, the teen culture was born.

CHILD LABOR LAWS PASSED
1934

US ENTERS WW II
1941

1929
THE GREAT DEPRESSION BEGINS

1940
TERM "TEENAGER" COINED

KINSEY STUDY REVEALS PREVALENCE OF HOMOSEXUALITY

1948

1944

SEVENTEEN MAGAZINE LAUNCHED

1954

SUPREME COURT BANS SEGREGATION IN PUBLIC SCHOOLS

THE
BLACK
SHEEP

MARC SCRUGGS

RANDOLPH SENIOR HIGH SCHOOL
RANDOLPH, OHIO
CLASS OF **1958**

He was born in Akron, but at age nine, his family moved to Randolph, a small, practically all-white farm community.

Marc came of age while the civil rights movement was gathering steam. In fact, as he entered his senior year, Little Rock, Arkansas, was attempting to integrate its schools amidst widespread protest.

Even though he was popular, a star of the football team, and his family was respected, he could not escape racism. The only person of color in his high school, Marc still remembers an encounter with a "well-meaning" teacher: "She asked me to come to her class; she just wanted to encourage me and tell me that I was well liked, and that nobody thought of me as a Negro."

Understanding the reality of the situation, Marc knew he could not escort a white girl from his class to his prom. Instead, he had to import a black girl from another town.

I ALWAYS KNEW THAT I WAS LOOKED AT as being different, and that I was different. I also knew they didn't know how different; men were the focal point of the world for me, and I knew that at four, clearly. I also knew that *that* was nothing to be said.

So, the growing up "different"—it's hard sometimes to know which part was the most significant. Was it because I was gay or because I was black that I became extremely arrogant in high school?

"I was emerging in this period of major social change and so I took it upon myself to affect change with my class."

Well some people thought it was arrogance; I think I was just pushy. I was emerging in this period of major social change and so I took it upon myself to affect change within my class. Things like, at graduation I insisted that my minister from Akron be the minister for baccalaureate. And I vaguely remember saying something like, "I've listened to your white preachers, and I think it's time you listen to mine."

And this was not a liberal town: I didn't know at the time, but in the '20s there was a revival of the Klan and anti-Semitism and anti-Catholicism in Randolph. And the Catholic portion of the town was burned down.

But I think I was able to do what I did because of the times: in the '50s there was marching going on, and there was all this talk from black soldiers about, "I fought and died for you in the war. I fought those evil people that you hated so much. So where's my house?" Because these soldiers were coming home after World War II—having

The woman working there said, "We don't allow *your* people in here." And I'm going, "Whose people?"

had the experience in Europe, particularly France, of being treated equally—but they couldn't get jobs here. So they hit the streets.

I did encounter opposition. When I was a freshman, I would go on Saturday mornings to the Summit Beach skating rink. Because that was what black kids did, that was the only time they went. I was aware of that, but it wasn't like a big deal. During Christmas vacation, there was a skating party sponsored by our class. And so I went to the party and it was great. Then, during the holiday break, a bunch of kids from school were going and asked if I wanted to go along.

When we got to the rink, they wouldn't let me in. The woman working there said, "I can't sell you a ticket," or something like that. I got out of line and went back and told some friends.

And they go, "Hmm, that's weird." So I got back in line, and then it happened again, and she said, "We don't allow *your* people in here." And I'm going, "Whose people?"—knowing and not knowing what she meant.

My dad had to come and get me. And that's the first time I ever saw him cry. He was just so frustrated, because he knew the man that owned the place. The man owned both the skating rink and the coal yard, and my dad always bought his coal there and had been doing so for years; they had this relationship. But the man said he just couldn't do it—that "the public wouldn't allow it" and the whole nine yards—and that the reason I had gotten in the other time was because it was a private party.

So, this was the first time that my dad really had to let me know that *this* was the world I was growing up in. He was a Southerner and so, for him, there must have been tons of shit going on in his head: that he hadn't done *whatever* to make this world a different place for me. Because that's one of the reasons we moved to the farm in the first place: so I wouldn't have to face that stuff.

But the upshot is that after he took me home, word got around and kids left the skating rink and boycotted it for months. I don't know why they did it. I think it was the best part of what that teacher meant when she said, "We don't think of you as a Negro." You know, that you're one of us.

Still, there was nobody for me to go to prom with. Remember, Emmett Till was my age. He was hung in the South in 1954; his crime was that he flirted with this white woman. It turned out the whole thing was a sham, that he had been hung totally without reason. So, I understood . . . I didn't understand, but I knew what I had to do. That if I wanted to go to the prom, I had to find somebody from another town.

The most logical place was through my church, which was in Akron. The first girl I asked, who I had a crush on, couldn't go because her family was Baptist enough that they didn't go to dances and do that sort of thing.

I also had a crush on this older women Clarissa, who was out of high school; she must have been a couple of years older. I asked her for her phone number in church and I called her and told her that I'd really like to take her to my prom and that, because I lived out in the country, she would stay over.

LEFT MARC STANDS OUT IN FIFTH GRADE **ABOVE** MARC WITH
FRIENDS ON GRADUATION DAY **RIGHT** OFFICIAL PROM
INVITE **PREVIOUS PAGES** MARC AND CLARISSA AT THE PROM;
MARC AT FIVE

The Junior Class
of Randolph High School
requests the honor of your presence at the
Annual Junior-Senior Prom
to be held
on Saturday, the fourth day of May
nineteen hundred and fifty-seven
from seven o'clock
until eleven-thirty in the evening
Twin Lakes Country Club
Twin Lakes, Ohio

r.s.v.p.

It's funny, when I asked Clarissa to the prom, I remember thinking that I would have rather taken her brother.

Clarissa was wonderful. From the minute I asked her, she basically made it all happen, she made it all work. She gave me the illusion that she was thinking it over and that it was a date for us. I mean, clearly it was out of that realm: she was doing a nice thing for a kid.

My parents liked her. She was very acceptable: she came from a nice family and she was an attractive young woman and very together. That she was an older woman was inconsequential, I mean, everybody understood what was happening here: that I was not going to get a date with anybody in town. My mother was always practical about those things.

I suspect they were just glad I was going with a girl; they didn't think I would go with a boy, but, you know, in the back of their minds, I think they knew what was going on. I'm sure my mother knew. She confronted me when I was fifteen. I went away to camp, but I had some boy magazines, like *Adonis* and whatnot, and I had put them under my bed at home. And she had made my bed and changed the room, and there were my *Adonis* magazines. So when I came home from camp, I can remember coming down the hall, and my mother asking, "Are you looking for something? I know what's going on." I denied it. But when we opened them up and there were these sticky pages, it was like, "Uh . . ."

She gave them back to me. And I had the feeling that I was supposed to destroy them, but I didn't. Just acquiring those magazines was like a fucking big deal. I'd go to the drugstore in Akron around the corner from my grandmother's. And they would be out on the magazine racks. I would stay for hours, and it never got any better. Each time I bought one, I'd be terrified to take them up to the counter. They were supposed to be just about physiques and stuff, but I was sure that whoever sold them would know. And that was still a time when people called people; I was worried that the owner would call my grandmother and say, "Do you know your grandson's up here buying *Adonis* magazines?"

It's funny, when I asked Clarissa to the prom, I remember thinking that I would have rather taken her brother. And there were several other

LEFT MARC AND HIS EX-WIFE IN A DRESS HE DESIGNED
RIGHT MARC WITH HARRY AND HIS SON FROM
HIS FIRST MARRIAGE

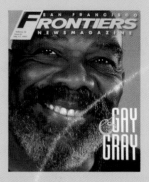

guys that I liked to be around. But I understood that there was something wrong with that. And that I could get in trouble if I let it go beyond that thought.

The prom. Oh, it was cool. One of my classmates, she had an older boyfriend who drove. And we double dated and went with them to the prom. And I'm sure I was drooling over him: he was old enough to have sideburns—that was a dream—and he had hair on his arms.

White dinner jackets were the call, but we were moving into that rebel period when we did wild things. I think I wore a powder-blue or pink jacket. That was non-traditional, but it was so hip. It was more like what colored people would do. This is an era when we're first starting to hear black music crossover. Kids in my school—not me, it was just the hip couples—would drive to Detroit to hear black music, because that's where it was happening. So those sounds and the kinds of outfits those guys wore were just beginning to filter down.

Clarissa wore a 1950s thing with lots of crinoline; it was strapless and she had a little jacket. I just sort of remember being the center of attention. It was cool: I had this good-looking young woman on my arm, so I could present; I could be who I was supposed to be. And, of course, she could dance—and you know what they say . . .

The music was rock-and-roll. We set a precedent: we were the first class to have a rock-and-roll band. And there was some slow music, because we were still in the midst of that period when musics were blended—old music, you know. So we were still doing songs that our parents did.

And I remember a big mirrored ball and all of the lights and dots. It did move, but believe me, there was no sense that there was a disco going on here—by any means.

The prom was at a "country club"; in this case, what it meant was it was in the country. One room overlooked a lake and we had dinner there. And of course everybody had been prepped for the dinner, with the idea that you had to eat dainty; you had to eat before you went to the dinner so that you left something on your plate.

Looking back , this was our coming out party. And it was like a class where we were supposed to learn how to dress up, and know how to attire yourself in this foreign garb. Every male was going, "I'm not going to wear a tux." Me? Honey, I couldn't wait. If I couldn't get that fucking crinoline gown, I was definitely going to get that tux.

Eventually, he did get that crinoline—sort of. "When I got married, I ended up designing my wife's wedding gown. Everybody should have known I was gay then; I should have known at that point."

Of course, on some level he knew he was "different" since he was four. So, why marry a woman? "Common knowledge of the day was that it was a passing phase and that all you needed to do was settle down and get married and raise a family," explains Marc, who does have a son from that marriage. "I would like to think that if things had been different I would not put somebody into that situation for my benefit."

Now in his sixties, Marc sees that his sexuality and his skin color have presented different challenges: "Being black, that wasn't something that I needed to handle, it was out there. I certainly had to deal with things; the family lore was, 'Always remember that you are representing your race.' But having to hide my sexuality, especially when I reached the point where the hormones were flowing, was particularly difficult."

"In retrospect, I'm *so* glad that I'm black; I am *so* glad that I'm gay and that those two things make me different," says Marc, a lifelong progressive activist. "Because if you're different, you can't afford to just walk through life without examining a lot of stuff."

THERESA IORIO*

WALT WHITMAN HIGH SCHOOL
LONG ISLAND, NEW YORK
CLASS OF **1958**

To look at her now—sixty-plus, sassy and vaguely flirtatious with a funky gray bob—you would never guess what she's been through.

She married her prom date Raymond and had two kids with him; twenty years later they divorced and she came out. As is the case with many lesbians who came of age in the '50s, the contours of Theresa's life seem to be shaped by cultural forces beyond her control.

A private person—"What can I say? I'm from the old school"—she asked that her real name and those of her family and friends not be used.

This cloak of anonymity freed her to speak openly about life before Stonewall, the Pill and Women's Lib.

* names and locations altered to ensure anonymity

THE VIRGIN MOTHER

I DIDN'T REALLY DATE IN HIGH SCHOOL, because I knew that I was a lezzie. When I went through puberty, I started looking at all of the girls and not the boys. I used to comment to all my little friends: "Look at the bust on that one." One day one friend said to me, "Oh, you sound just like a guy." And I said to myself, "Uh oh, I better shut up; something's going on here with me."

I met Raymond through my best friend; her name was Anne. Now, I was madly in love with her, of course. And she met this guy by the name of Chuck. When she used to go with him I felt terrible, left out and devastated. After six months, she said, "Would you like to double-date with us? With Chucky and his friend Ray?" I said, "Oh yes."

I would have gone with anybody—the Phantom of the Opera—just to be with her. But she said, "Oh, but you have to see if you like him first." So I went to this club, and Ray was there with Chuck. And she said, "That's him right there; that's Ray so-and-so." I said, "Oh, okay."

So we started double-dating and double-dating. We double-dated for a while, until Raymond started saying, "We don't need them." *Now what do I do?* So I said, "I guess." I was so inexperienced, so dumb. He started pressuring me for sex. And I was just a nice, little Catholic girl from Brooklyn. I said, "Oh no, I could never do that, because I have to get married first."

I graduated high school in June of '58. The prom was, I guess, right before that. I was still a virgin at that point. I asked Raymond to go, and I think we double-dated with Anne. Now I don't know if she went with Chuck. I cannot remember; it's over forty-five years ago.

Raymond had a brand-new Ford Crestline convertible with a Continental wheel in the back. It had a red-leather interior. If I'm not mistaken, he picked me up in that.

The prom was in the auditorium or the gym. And I guess the music was the '50s rock-and-roll. 1958, it'd have to be. I used to listen to that stuff on forty-fives. So it had to be the '50s rock-and-roll. My dress was blue, like a light, icy blue. And it was strapless. And I think I had a little shawl over my shoulders, but very light, very sheer. And I wore a tiara and got my hair done in a French twist, which was very bizarre. It was almost like I was a dressed-up tomboy. It was surreal, like I was on some sort of cloud.

Raymond was in a tuxedo; it looked good. We danced a little bit, but not too much—he didn't really dance—just a little bit for show. To me, prom was like an obligation. If people didn't go to their prom, there was something wrong with them, you know?

> One night, I was in the backseat with him, and he did something to me. It was like *boop* and I was like, "What was that?"

I don't remember what we did after the prom. I feel like we went someplace, but I have no idea where. In those days, we used to do this making out in the car. We would just drive to some desolate spot, usually by the water, and park the car and steam up all of the windows.

For six months after we started dating, I did not do anything, just making out. So he kept saying, "Oh, we should do this" and "Oh, I love you." All this baloney. Then one night, I was in the backseat with him, and he did something to me. I didn't even know what happened; it was like *boop.* And I was like, "What was that?"

So that happened again. And I got pregnant. Yes I did; I got pregnant. I missed some periods, and then I told my mother—this is in the '50s, so this is bad—"I think I have a growth in my stomach, because I didn't get my period in four months." She said, "What? Oh you're going to the doctor."

So I go with my mother, and the doctor gives me an examination and he's turning white. He said, "Tumor? Your daughter is four months pregnant." That was the beginning of the end.

I went home, and my mother said, "Wait until your father hears this." My father is a Sicilian, born in Sicily, and my mother's Italian too. And nothing ever happened like this with their family; they got married in a nice way. My father went crazy. They said, "Oh, you're gonna get married." I said, "Married? I'm not gonna marry him; I don't even know him. And I don't love him." And they said, "But you're having a baby. You're gonna marry him or you're gonna go into a home." So I said, "Well, I'm going into a home, because I'm not gonna marry him."

The "home" is a home for unwed mothers. That's what they did in the archaic '50s. They said, "You can go there, and you can live

On the dance floor, after we got married, do you know what Raymond whispered in my ear?

"The party's over."

there until you have the baby; and then you give the baby up for adoption."

I don't know how many months I stayed there, maybe four. And my parents really didn't support me. I used to call them up on a pay phone and say, "I want to come home; I don't like it here."

The home was run by nuns, and they told me, "When you're ready to have the baby, you'll start to have pains and you'll tell us right away, and we'll take you to St. Vincent's Hospital." So when it was time I told the nuns, and they came and said, "Okay, call your parents and tell them you're going to the hospital. We'll call a social worker, and she'll take you down there."

They kept telling me in the home, "You'll never see the baby, because it's very cruel. You just have the baby, sign the papers and go home; nobody will ever know."

After I had the baby, I was in like a big dormitory. And I'm looking around, and I see in the distance this nurse is coming towards me. In those days, the nurses wore a white cap. And she's coming toward me with this baby, a big baby with black hair. And she's coming towards me and coming and coming. She comes right up to me and says, "Do you want to breast-feed or use the bottle?" Can you believe this? I'm all by myself, and I'm looking at my baby, who is my son Raymond Jr. Eight pounds, thirteen ounces. All I said to her—I'll never forget this—"Give me the bottle, just give me the bottle."

I called my parents and said, "Look, I just saw the baby, and I'm not gonna give him up." And they said, "You crazy girl you, after all we went through with you." I said, "Look, I don't care. I can't listen to you anymore. I had the baby and I'm not giving him up and that's it."

My parents came to the hospital. I said to them, "Would you help me bring the baby home?" And they said, "No, we're not helping you, because the neighbors will find out that you have a baby."

So I called up Mr. Raymond. And I said, "Look, you and I have a child. You have to do the right thing by me, we have to get married." But he said, "I don't want to, because I'm too young." I said, "I feel the same way, but that's the only way we can keep the baby; my mother's not gonna help me, and I don't know how I'm gonna take care of the baby alone. You're gonna have to assume responsibility;

we're gonna have to get married. And that's the only way we can keep our son." He said, "Alright, I'll do it."

Then my parents decided that they didn't want their family to know that I had a baby before getting married, so I had to put in the paper that I was engaged. And then they planned this gigantic wedding. I listened to them, because at that point I felt very ashamed of myself. So I walked down the aisle and got married to Mr. Raymond Sr., and I had a baby at home. By then he was seven-months old, and nobody knew. On the dance floor, after we got married, do you know what Raymond whispered in my ear? "The party's over." He might as well have taken a knife and plunged it into my heart. It was like, "You made me marry you, now you're gonna pay."

The marriage lasted for over twenty years. I was so afraid of getting pregnant that I was like a crazy woman; I don't know how this happened, but I had another child, my daughter Margaret, which, thank God I have her too. She's a teacher in L.A.; and Raymond Jr. is a lawyer, and he works in Manhattan.

But it was a loveless marriage. He did not have any interest in the house, he did not have any interest in me, and he did not have any interest at all in the children. What a shame, because he has two beautiful children. He was just in his own world. I used to call him the Star Border. He was a good provider, but that's it.

And my crushes never stopped. I belonged to a lot of groups — I call myself a group animal. I was in a photography club and art groups for years and years. Always with women. And, do you know, I never cheated on him in all those twenty years, not even once.

In the late '70s, I was going so out of my mind that I had to come out. I was a member of NOW for several years. And I decided to speak to this woman Lisa, who was in charge of the Lesbian Task Force for my chapter.

I said, "Look, I've been trying to come out for years. I don't know what to do. I don't know where to go, who to speak to. I'm afraid to even say the word 'lesbian.'" She said, "I'll help you. And did you know there's a lesbian bar in your town that's been there for nine years?" *Nine* years.

I came out to my friend Ronnie, who I'd been in love with for years. She was the wife of one of my husband's friends, like an ex-Marine buddy. And she really didn't think anything of my coming out. She probably thought I was just kidding or something.

Then I said to Ronnie, "You have to go to this bar with me." She said, "Listen, you and I have been through a lot of crazy stuff over the years" — you know, a lot of pranks, antics — "but this is too much. I'm not going to go to a lesbian bar with you." But I talked her into it.

We went, and we saw the owner there. Her name was Marie, and she was watching hockey and drinking beer; and she had all of these keys hanging off her and lots of pinkie rings. And there were all of these other dykey women with loud mouths.

And my friend Ronnie says, "This is what you want? Oh, I feel sorry for you. This is what you want?" And I said, "Uh, I don't, uh, I, uh. . . yeah. Yeah."

POSTSCRIPT

Soon thereafter, Theresa came out to her family. Even though she began dating women, she and her husband continued to live together for several years. Theresa remembers, "He said, 'You can stay here. You do your thing, and I'll do mine; I got used to you after all these years.'"

She didn't leave until she met Eleanor. "I was so happy to get away from him, and to be on my own and support myself, and to have Eleanor sleep next to me every night." Theresa and Eleanor stayed together for more than ten years.

Theresa, who still lives on Long Island, was thrilled to read about a local gay prom in the newspaper recently. "If I was seventeen now and I was out — and I think I would have been — I would have been excited about going," she says.

"I was very tomboyish," she adds. "And now when I go to these senior lesbian groups, these big butches think of me as a big femme. But I would have been the little butch in a tuxedo asking out one of my little girl-friends to the gay prom."

THE LATE
BLOOMER

DICK HEWETSON

ROOSEVELT HIGH SCHOOL
MINNEAPOLIS, MINNESOTA
CLASS OF **1948**

"I have lived two lives," says the former Episcopal priest. "And when I look back on that life, it's almost like I see myself in the third person, like it's someone else."

In 1972, Dick officially left the church and came out. Three years later, he met his first partner David, a semi-closeted teacher ten years his senior, and the two became elder statesmen in the gay community of Minnesota's Twin Cities.

Together, they fought orange juice pitchwoman Anita Bryant's homo-hating campaign to repeal Saint Paul's gay anti-discrimination laws. And with their own money, Dick and David founded one of the first queer lending libraries in the country, at a time when serious gay novels were easier to find in "adult" bookstores than Barnes & Noble.

In 1981, more than thirty years after his own high school prom, Dick also helped organize a prom for gay adults. "There's one way the two proms *didn't* differ," he jokes, "I couldn't dance at either."

T HE WHOLE CONCEPT OF COMING OUT is a '70s idea. If you grew up in the '50s, and somebody asked you if you've come out to anybody, you wouldn't even know what they meant.

Back then, my parents were friends with a gay male couple, and we used to go visit them. One of them did needlepoint, which my mother and my aunt used to giggle about. But the thing is: you didn't talk about it. It was there, but nobody ever mentioned it; it was kind of don't ask, don't tell.

> "I went and talked to the priest, because I realized it's time just to admit that I'm gay and try to figure out what it all means."

When I think back, those two men, who were really nice guys, probably had me figured out. But I never dealt with my sexuality; I lived a totally sexless life until I was in my forties.

In the early 1970s, suddenly I began hearing things about gay people. The gay movement started making news and, of course, it was very controversial. People had all of these weird ideas: that homosexuals were all in some underworld, where they were up to no good or whatever.

Dick Hewetson

At the time I was working in a church on Sundays. And I went and talked to the priest, because I realized it was time just to admit that I'm gay, and try to figure out what it all meant. Well, this priest took me down to this place called Gay House, which was a drop-in center.

It's interesting that at that point, in Minnesota, they already had a gay drop-in center. Unfortunately, it was an awful place, just an old, run-down house. And I was forty-two-years-old, and all of the people there were under twenty-three and most of them were strung out on drugs; I just didn't feel like I belonged.

But one day at Gay House, they announced there was going to be a speaker at the University's Episcopal church, of all places. The speaker was Barbara Gittings and I thought, Hah, I can go there because it's the Episcopal church and people will think I'm just a

> # I got really involved politically before I ever had any sexual experience.

priest who's interested. Well, she was the first gay person that I ever heard speak who really had something to say. And she was so self-assured and so okay with being gay. After her speech, they announced that there was going to be a meeting of the Minnesota Committee for Gay Rights, and I went to that.

It's weird, I got really involved politically before I ever had any sexual experience. Almost overnight, I became a gay activist. And I finally found a way to connect with some gay people who were closer to my age. And had a goal.

Back then, the main concern was employment and housing. But more so employment, because the minute somebody was found out to be gay, they would lose their job. I actually testified at the city council in Saint Paul for the gay rights ordinance in 1974.

When I got up to testify, I asked the press not to identify me, because I wasn't out on the job. On the evening news, they showed me testifying, but they showed my back. The next day at work, people walked by me and said, "You have a very photogenic back." It went fine; as often happens, my fear was a lot worse than reality.

I had already planned to come out to my sister, but after this experience at work, I thought, You better not stall this any longer. So I went to her house, and we sat out in her yard. There had been a documentary on TV around that time about a gay couple and a lesbian couple; and I said to her, "I don't know if you caught it, but there was a thing on the news, and I was in it." So she said, "Oh, was that that thing about the gay couples?" And I said, "No, but I was testifying at the city council about a gay rights ordinance."

She was perfectly okay with it. She was actually relieved, because she thought I was coming to tell her that I was moving away and that she was going to have to take care of our dad. And then she told me that when she was in high school—she graduated in '53—she used to chum around with the gay guys. I still find this amazing; I didn't know there were any gay guys. I think the whole idea was so terrifying to me that I wouldn't have noticed. But this is my sister the fag hag. In fact, she would much rather spend time with gay people than I would. There are some gay people that focus on everything gay; it gets so boring. And all of the innuendos and silly things they say—after you've heard them fifty times, they're not funny any more.

But the reason I thought about it is that, when I came out to her, my sister said, "I only have one question: what about Betty?" Well, Betty was the girl I took to the prom. I met her in a ballroom-dancing class when I was sixteen-years-old. I went with a buddy of mine, who has turned out to be gay, of course. He and I went to learn to dance, because you had to take out girls and you had to know how to dance.

By the time prom came, Betty already had a diamond from me: it was an engagement ring. She missed her period and decided she was pregnant. Which she couldn't have possibly been; we did a lot of kissing and hugging and feeling, but we never had any sex.

But I was so naïve and I was scared to death. And at that point in history, you know, you had to do the right thing and you had to get married. And the thing to do was to quickly get a ring and pretend that you were just engaged. We eventually broke up; I mean, she wasn't pregnant—after a while you find these things out. And after we broke up, her dad kidnapped me, in a sense, to try and get me back for Betty.

He really liked me; he thought I was a catch. In fact, I probably drove his car to the prom. My family didn't have a car, and when I was sixteen, Betty's dad paid for me to take driving lessons so I could have a driver's license and use his car.

I can't tell you what Betty wore to prom; can't tell you what I wore either. I know I got her a corsage, because that's also what you did.

I know that we must have danced. I may have tried to lindy hop. That was *the* dance that people did; it was sort of the follow-up to the jitterbug. I'm sure they also played some waltzes and fox trots—that sort of traditional ballroom dancing stuff.

I remember my second prom a little better. It was in 1981, and I went with my lover David. At that time, I was the president of the Out & About Theater, a gay theater in Minneapolis. We got the idea that, for a fundraiser, we would have a prom since none of us had ever really had that prom experience.

It was held at an old mansion that had become a women's club. We got a band, we hired a photographer, somebody did the most wonderful poster, and we had a prom. And I remember a couple of lesbians that came: Dorothy in this long, flowy red dress and Jackie in a tuxedo. It was just a riot!

THAT PROM.

OUR PROM.

THE PROM WITH A DIFFERENCE.
at The Blaisdell Place
2322 Blaisdell Avenue, Minneapolis

Saturday May 8
8 pm and into the night

Disco — Cash Bar — Food — Continuous Entertainment
Tickets: $12.00 in advance, $15.00 at the door. Mail order tickets
available by sending check and self-addressed stamped envelope to
Out and About Theatre, 512 Nicollet Mall, Mpls., MN 55402

ABOVE DAVID AND DICK PROTESTING THE ANITA BRYANT-INSPIRED REFERENDUM IN 1978
LEFT A POSTER FOR THE GAY PROM

For all the talk about how awful the Midwest is, I lived a very openly gay life in Saint Paul for twenty years. I was respected by lots and lots of people. And David and I were seen as a couple.

I was just back there, because David and I were given lifetime recognition awards for having started the Quatrefoil Library in 1983. Back in the '80s, finding gay books was not easy. And David was a bookworm. Wherever we went, he would go to used bookstores and he would find these gems. We eventually had 1,500 books, plus all of these newspapers we sub-scribed to from all over the country; and our friends would borrow them. Well, it all sort of took over our condominium, so we came up with this idea that we would set up this lending library. And we did. And it now has 9,000 books; I think it's the second largest gay lending library in the country.

David and I were together until 1984. We are still very good friends; we're in touch, now particularly with email. We have a very special relationship because of all of the things we did together. And we never had a falling out; in fact, I don't remember ever having an argument with him. But we just sort of grew apart; we just became two people liv-ing in the same house. What's interesting is, during the period that we were still living together and selling our condominium, he said to me, "You know, we had five wonderful years together." And I thought, Isn't that interesting? Because we were together for eight years. But I thought, That's just about right.

The first five years were wonderful, and that's when you see us in our prom picture. That's the point in our lives that we were really, really happy together. It's funny, from the moment I decided I wanted to deal with being gay, all I wanted was a lover. All I wanted was a relation-ship with somebody. He was fifty-five and I was forty-five when we met. The fact that we had finally found somebody and we formed this rela-tionship and bought this condominium together was really wonderful. And when I look at that picture, I think the grins on our faces say a lot.

In 1978, a referendum fueled by Anita Bryant's anti-gay rhetoric garnered a sixty-percent majority and essentially repealed the ordi-nance that Dick had help pass. "People were all upset and I said, 'Look, forty-percent of the voters are on our side!' At the time, I thought that was pretty fantastic."

Times have clearly changed: Dick now lives in San Francisco and met his present lover of six years online. And while job discrimination still exists, "the surprise," says Dick, "is that we discuss things like gay marriage. They were just way off the radar screen years ago. And the thing I see is that the society, as a whole, is okay with gay people; they're much more okay with gay people than they are with a lot of other things."

These days, Dick stays out of gay politics, but he's hardly apolitical. He's an outspoken pro-ponent of the separation of state and church. And while he considers himself "a retired activist," Dick continues to pen letters to the edi-tor, speak at atheist conventions and picket overt displays of religion in public spaces.

BOB TURCO

FENTON HIGH SCHOOL
FENTON, MICHIGAN
CLASS OF **1943**

A seventy-five-year-old World War II veteran and retired airline executive, Bob grew up in a small, conservative town outside of Flint, Michigan. Because "my brother was the mayor of the town for many years, I had to be careful what I said or did."

He now resides in Queens and is one of the more lively members of the local chapter of Senior Action in a Gay Environment (SAGE), a social club for lesbian and gay seniors. Along with a dozen or so regulars, Bob hangs out a few afternoons a week and engages in the usual mix of reminiscing, politics, innuendoes and small talk.

Recently, he helped plan the group's Senior Prom social, which attracted more than eighty of his peers.

I WAS POPULAR IN SCHOOL. I was the president of my class my sophomore and senior years. I was on the football team and ran track. Anyone that didn't participate in sports was a "fairy" or a "cocksucker." I remember in school, a couple of guys were very effeminate. I just felt so sorry for them; no one would bother with them. My God, they were just taunted night and day.

> "Of course, I sent her a corsage. You sent it in those days."

I had girlfriends then, quite a lot of girlfriends. I don't think anything was ever serious, as far as any really heavy romantic interest. It was just dating a girl because that was one of the codes: if you didn't date, there was probably something wrong with you, so the establishment said.

My prom date's name was Bethany. She was a very popular girl, she was very pretty, she was very tall, exquisite looking. We went together off and on for two or three years. I asked her a few months before prom, because I knew if I didn't, someone would beat me to it. She wanted to go with me because I was tall and she was tall; she didn't want to overwhelm the situation. And she could wear high-heeled shoes.

Of course, I sent her a corsage. You sent it in those days. I picked her up; I had my dad's car. And I picked up another couple, and the four of us went together. It was a typical prom night: you went to the local ice cream parlor and had a coke—the primary reason you went there was to show off your date—and then you went to the school and you danced.

I don't remember if we had a live orchestra or just records. In those days, the records were the big seventy-eights. They were huge and you only had one song on one record. Somebody had to be there to turn it over or put on a new record. Anyway, you danced the night away.

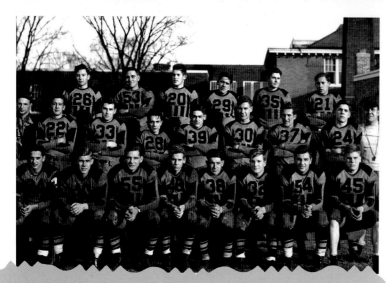

You were even careful what you wore, because you didn't want to be labeled a "faggot." And God help you if you were caught with white shoes.

It was the Big Band era then—the Dorseys, Glenn Miller. You did a little bit of jitterbugging, but at a prom you did more romantic steps. And you always had a grand march, too. Afterwards, you went out to a local restaurant where everybody else went, and you had something to eat and drink until twelve, one o'clock in the morning. Then you went out and necked for an hour or so. And then you drove around and went to another necking spot and you necked some more. Then you took the girl home. It was about three or four in the morning. I didn't have sex on prom night, but she played with me.

When I did have sex with a woman, I didn't enjoy it; it wasn't fulfilling. I don't know if I had an inkling I was gay at that time. I knew that I was different; I was attracted to men.

But I always suppressed that desire by hanging out with females and enjoying female company. Because, in those days, it wasn't done. At all. You were a freak if you were gay. You were even careful what you wore, because you didn't want to be labeled a "faggot." You never wore a sleeveless shirt, and you never had long hair. Even if you grew a beard, you were labeled a "faggot" or a "queer" or a "cocksucker." And God help you if you were caught with white shoes. There were so many things like that. You never wore rings. Never, never, never. And you never wore a bracelet, because you'd be labeled a "queer." Now, when I see a young guy with a bracelet, I actually think, God, you're lucky.

I graduated high school in June of '43, and in December of '43 I was in the Navy—that's how fast the wheels turned in those days. Well, it was World War II time; the war was already on and they didn't give you time to enjoy civilian life.

I was worried about going in—I think everyone was—because you didn't know what was going to happen. You didn't know if you were going overseas or staying in the US. And my parents were really horrified by it, because my brother and I were both in the service.

I really enjoyed being in the Navy. Whereas so many gay guys that I've talked to through the years despised being in the service, that wasn't me at all. I suppose because they were more aware of their sexuality than I was. Because in those days, I used to look at women, and men too. Aboard ship, you had to shower with sometimes ten or twelve men, and you would see them, and you would just sort of linger in the shower after they left, hanging on 'til the next group came in. You were looking everybody over and, at the same time, you were wondering what the hell was going on in your mind. At night, you were in your bunk, it was two or three tiers high, and you used to watch all of the guys sleeping, seeing—if I can be candid—you were always looking around to see if any of them were getting a hard-on. But you didn't dare touch anyone. If you even touched anyone, you were court marshalled immediately. And it was extremely difficult because, even if you suppressed your thoughts, they would come back to you because of the very atmosphere of being around 200 or 300 men all the time.

ABOVE BOB'S HIGH SCHOOL FOOTBALL TEAM (HE'S IN THE FRONT ROW, SECOND FROM THE RIGHT) **RIGHT** WITH FRIENDS AT THE PROM

> # I first heard the term "gay." I asked a lesbian next to me, "What does that mean?" And she said, "Well, that's what we are."

I'm sure quite a few of them had the same feeling that I had, because you would catch a fleeting glance of men glancing at one another. You just knew there was an unwritten message there: they were probably, or hopefully, thinking the same thing you were. You knew you wanted to get together with them, but it was an impossible situation. So you would usually find a spot to jerk off to relieve the pressure. And you had a masturbation image when you jerked off; you jerked off thinking about somebody in ship's company.

The first time I acted on the impulse was near discharge time, and we were going to Portland, Oregon, to decommission the ship. We all got a twelve-hour leave and I went to a movie by myself. Some of the other guys wanted me to go with them, but I didn't because I was going to steal a chance to maybe make it. I went to a movie, and I found a lone guy sitting there. I sat down next to him and eventually we started rubbing knees, and then he put his hand on my knee. But that's as far as it went. Then he got up and went to the back of the lobby. And I got up and went back there, and we started talking. He was staying at a hotel, and he invited me up to his hotel room. I wasn't even sure what was going to happen—I know what I wanted to happen—and then we got up there and it did happen. I don't know if I was any good in those days or not; it was a frightening experience, but I was glad it happened. Then I went back to the ship. A month later, we were discharged.

I bummed around the country for a while and then I went to Chicago. That was really when I came out. In the '50s, you weren't out completely. You went back and forth into the closet. I would come out of the closet for a night and go back in the next day, and stay in two or three days, and go back out. In and out, in and out.

You would seek out the gay bars for your own kind, to have somebody to feel comfortable with. You knew it wouldn't last, because there would be a raid. I was in so many goddamned raids. Every time you went into a bar, there was the risk that it would be raided, and invariably it was.

And the cops were so ugly to you. They would call you all sorts of filthy, rotten names. Degrade you. Kick you in the ass when they put you in the paddy-wagon. I used to get so vindictive; I wanted to go back and shoot them. "Fuckin' cocksucker," they'd say, "get in there. You want to suck my dick. Fuckin' queers, you oughta be shot." Then you'd go to the station house and they'd put you all in one big holding pen and just taunt you all night long. And the judge the next day would have the same attitude. He wouldn't say it, but it was, "Okay queers, back on the streets."

My favorite club in Chicago was Shoreline 7. It was down a dark alley and, of course, there was no neon sign flashing on and off; there was just a painted sign over the door. There was just drinking, no dancing or anything like that, no movies, nothing that would lead anybody to believe it was a gay bar. That was where I first heard the term "gay." I asked a lesbian next to me, I asked, "Well, what does that mean?" And she said, "Well, that's what we are. We are gay. This is a gay bar, and we're part of the gay community."

In those days there was no such thing as a gay political organization. There were no support groups. And so many gay people had really difficult times adjusting to being gay. Even psychiatrists thought it was a mental illness. I had counseling for over three years; that didn't help because the therapist, he took the stand that others did: that we had mental problems. The therapist tried to cure me of being gay by painting such a horrible picture of it, saying that it wasn't accepted and the only acceptable lifestyle was to get married and raise a family. They just drummed that into you. I used to ask him questions about the gay life, and he'd say, "Why do you ask me?" For chrissakes, I asked him because I wanted an answer, but I never got one.

The Stonewall riots: that spawned the gay community. When it happened, I think every gay person in the country was rooting for them. The papers were full of nothing but that on the front-page, about how the drag queens tipped over squad cars and threw rocks at the cops. You wanted to be there with them, you didn't care what happened, you just wanted to be there throwing bricks and stones. And you wanted to say, "You bastards, I'm not crazy. I'm just a gay human being."

That was the opening I needed and so many other people needed. *Here I am; I'm gay and I'm not crazy.* And then I just made up my mind that I was going to live comfortably and happy. I went to gay bars; I went to gay restaurants with friends. It was a freedom, a sexual freedom. *At last, my God, here we are. Why didn't it happen years ago?*

It hasn't been easy for any of the people I've known through the years that are gay. A couple of them are so bitter, so resentful. One guy here at SAGE resents the heterosexual world for his fate in life: he's well past the retirement age, but he still has to clean apartments; he was an alcoholic for years because, he said, "I'd drink myself into oblivion and forget about being gay until I woke up the next morning."

I have a lot of straight friends—the things they have said to me through the years. They're more tolerant now; they understand it more. They used to have the stereotype impression that we all walked like women and wore makeup and wore women's clothes. That's all changed.

Through the years, Bob and his prom date have maintained a close relationship. "We still talk to one another once or twice a year. She always sends me invitations to her children's birthdays or to her anniversary."

In fact, Bethany and her family have visited Bob in New York and he's shown them all over the city. He hasn't come out to her. "But she suspects," says Bob, "because she's not a stupid woman."

And if she asked him now? "I would say, 'Yes.'"

ABOVE BOB (TOP LEFT) AND HIS NAVY BUDDIES RELAX WHILE ON LEAVE

THE
IMMORTAL
SOUL

MARINSKA DOLNAR

EVANDER CHILDS HIGH SCHOOL
BRONX, NEW YORK
CLASS OF **1935**

With gray hair and a tiny frame that's slightly stooped, she looks like the stereotypical little old lady. But even the briefest of conversations reveals a fiercely intelligent and independent spirit who has bucked convention from the get go: on the back of a motorcycle; in a long-term relationship with another woman; as a senior who studies Kabbalah.

Still, Marinska carries the baggage of a generation that rarely spoke the word "lesbian" and pre-dated "bisexual," a generation that compartmentalized sexuality out of necessity. "During my fifty-five years with my friend, I was married all of those years," she explains. "Both of my husbands knew that I was with her. And she knew that I was with them. That was the only way I could do it; I couldn't go through my life lying. So I tried to explain to each of them that this was two separate lives; although this person is the same physical body, it was as if I were two people with two completely different lifestyles and two different sets of values and needs."

On her eighty-fifth birthday, this acclaimed journalist published her superb first novel, *To Mine Own Selves Be True*, under the nom de plume Marinska Dolnar. She employs that name once again to maintain her anonymity. "I'm comfortable talking about anything at all," she notes, "as long as you don't use my real name."

I WENT TO EVANDER CHILDS HIGH SCHOOL in the Bronx, which then was a glitteringly new school building. And today I'm told it's one of the biggest slum high schools in town. My classmates were both poor Italians and poor Jews. The poor Jews I knew mostly about, because they all lived in my building.

The young people that I hung out with were either Zionists or Communists. If you weren't one, you were the other. And it you weren't either, you were just one of the *schnooks* who didn't have a mind. You had to have a mind in order to be respected in our group. So, you see, we never gave a damn about prom. Because there were more important things—there certainly were.

> "You had to have a mind in order to be respected in our group. So, you see, we never gave a damn about prom."

When I graduated high school it was 1935. The word "prom" wasn't a part of our vocabulary; I mean, that was for rich people who lived on Park Avenue. There were no dances or anything like that in high school. I think it's because of the Depression. We couldn't afford dresses and the rest. We were just too poor.

The Depression came in 1929; by that time I was eleven-years-old. Before that, I only knew that my father made a living and that we weren't scared of anything and life was normal. But when the Depression struck, the effect was immediate. Like a bang on the head. Terribly traumatic.

People jumped off the George Washington Bridge, which had just then been finished. All of their money was wiped out overnight. And the people who were mostly hurt were the people who had already made their money and suddenly they didn't have it. People had expensive apartments and they had bought their furniture and their cars . . . and everything was bought on a down payment. And all of a sudden they couldn't make their payments; and they not only lost their cars, but they lost their apartments and they wound up in the street. Just like my parents did.

We were told about the junior prom and that Glenn Miller was going to play.

I came home from school one day and I found my mother and father standing on the sidewalk, and our furniture was there also on the sidewalk. It was horrible. Horrible. Somehow my mother and father found a room in somebody else's three-room apartment, which was a kitchen, living room and bedroom. And that family was just as badly hurt as we were; they were glad to rent out one of their rooms. They slept and lived and ate in their bedroom, and we slept and lived and ate in their former living room, which they cleaned out, and we put in my mother's and father's things.

How long did we live there? Years. Many years. Eventually, my father was able to get a little work, and my mother went out and went to night school and studied how to be a nurse's aide. My mother felt that anybody who had been a mother, and knows how to take care of children, could take care of anybody. So she became a nurse's aide. And my mother supported my father and me.

So we were poor, but we never talked about being poor. Because we lived in a neighborhood in the Bronx where everybody was poor; it was a way of life. It doesn't mean that we didn't have any fun. Oh we did. We had our own fun; not the kind of fun that comes with the prom. We would gather in each other's homes and have long-winded intellectual and political discussions on all of these subjects. We were very well educated; we were very aware of politics—and not only local politics, but also world politics and wars and all that. And we couldn't be without music, but it wasn't the music that you're thinking about. We would play all the Hebrew songs and we would dance a *hora* in the street . . . and we listened to classical music. But we had some popular dance music, too. I inherited a lot from my mother and father. They came from the Ukraine and Russia: a very, very, very bad place to come from for Jews; totally anti-Semitic, brutally so. But when they came here, they became interested in all of the Americanized things like danc-

ing. And I would sit up at night while my mother and father practiced in the kitchen, which was the only room that had a straight floor; you wouldn't dance on the rug, God forbid, because you could spoil the rug. They danced the fox trot, they danced the waltz, they danced a tango. And I remember watching them; they were just hilarious, because they didn't have the figures for it. But I didn't want to dance anything—it wasn't for me and all of my friends.

Actually, my first husband Marvin taught me how to dance the lindy, but very clumsily. I don't have a natural grace for that. He and I grew up in the Bronx together. We met one time in the country, and we found out that we both loved T.S. Eliot. And we still recite the same poem that we recited to each other the day we met: "Let us go then, you and I / When the evening is spread out against the sky / Like a patient etherized upon a table / Let us go, through certain half-deserted streets" . . . It's a beautiful poem.

After high school, I went to Hunter College, which in those days was free to anyone who had the high grades. I was a pre-med and I went through two years of Hunter. Marvin went to Iowa, of all places, to go to college. And I got lonesome for him. So I quit Hunter and went to Iowa to be with him and finish up school.

We got married to be able to be together. In those days, you didn't just say, "Ma and pa, I'm going to go live with what's-his-name." You had to get married. I mean, come on, What will the neighbors think? So we hitchhiked all the way to Woodstock, New York, and found a justice of the peace along the highway. And we handed him two dollars and he married us. And that was it.

Then we hitchhiked to college. And it was so strange, when I was finally in Iowa, to see myself surrounded by sororities and fraternities and students who were well-to-do, students whose parents paid their big bills and bought them beautiful clothes to wear. We had to work our way through, and we lived in a little room in town. And our life was being students and getting our homework done and trying to make it until graduation.

But when we finally came to our junior year, we were told about the junior prom and that Glenn Miller was going to play. And everybody was jumping up and down that we were going to have Glenn Miller for our prom. And I said to my husband, "Who the hell is Glenn Miller?" He said, "I don't know. He's some important jazz person or something." Because we were all strictly classical musicians; Bach was our thing, not Glenn Miller. We didn't care.

So you see, I'm a poor person to interview, because we were the intelligentsia. The intelligentsia just didn't think anything about prom or things like dances. When you hung out with these people, "idealism" was the word. Idealism is not Glenn Miller; idealism is not going to prom.

Marvin and I actually had an argument about going. He was forever in favor of the working class and he says, "What do you need that for? What does it mean? It means nothing; it's a bunch of bologna." And I knew that what he said was true, but I said, "Look, we're only young once; we're having an experience. A junior prom is something that we'll always remember." He grudgingly gave in. And the picture shows it.

We took the picture ourselves. In other words, we had it on a timer. We stood in our kitchen with a white sheet hanging behind us so the viewers wouldn't see a stove or a sink or something. And the result was something so funny. You could see how we were struggling. My husband was so stiff. And I've always been a tomboy, so that's the first time in my life that I ever wore a long dress.

Ten dollars was the price for everything I wore, including my handbag. We had five dollars a week to live on for food. And out of the five dollars, he spent, to my annoyance, one dollar on a carton of cigarettes. Chesterfields. And so that left us with only four dollars to live on. Then to go and spend ten dollars—two weeks worth of food—that was a fortune for us. And I consider that it looks hysterically funny and absurd, because underneath all that is a different kind of a person, a person who would not be caught dead wearing that kind of an outfit.

TO MINE OWN SELVES BE TRUE

A NOVEL BY

MARINSKA DOLNAR

By the time we got done taking the picture and shouting at each other to stand up straight, we were ready to say, "The hell with it; let's not go." And we didn't have a car or anything, so walked to the prom in our fancy clothes down across the campus. When we got there, everybody was so la-di-da, and we were so *not* la-di-da. And I was extremely uncomfortable. I didn't know how to dance these dances that people danced. Marvin was an excellent dancer; he made it work somehow for me. And he and I stuck to each other like glue because we didn't want to talk to anybody. I cannot say that I enjoyed it, but I have the memory of it. And what is our life but a memory of everything that we've experienced?

POSTSCRIPT

A year after the prom, during her senior year in Iowa, Marinska met an art student named Dot and fell in love. "I had never seen anyone who moved me and who, though I couldn't begin to explain it, was as heartbreakingly exciting as was this girl."

Says Marinska: "What I knew about lesbianism I got from the first book about lesbianism that I had ever read. It's called *The Well of Loneliness*. I read it in my early college days. It's so old fashioned in its approach, but that book opened my eyes up to something in me."

"The prospects for a lesbian or a homosexual to be out in those days were not there," she adds, "How out you were depended on how much you were willing to bear."

Marinska and Marvin eventually divorced, but the two are still close friends. "His reaction today is one of total understanding. And back then, as soon as he fell in love with another girl and married her, everything was fine."

In 1950, Marinska married a handsome Englishman that she met on Fire Island. But her relationship with Dot continued until Dot passed away in 1994. "We stayed together thanks to love letters, of which I have a vast amount stored away somewhere, and telephone calls, and about a half dozen meetings a year."

As she explains in her recent book, "Why must [one] make a choice? Bisexuality . . . is a natural state. It may manifest, if allowed to, wherever love from the heart or perhaps from the soul may lead one, for surely the immortal soul has no gender."

Having never conformed to the roles prescribed by society, it's not surprising that Marinska embraces the gray area between homo and hetero—a concept many young queers are just beginning to contemplate.

GLOSSARY

ACT UP
Acronym: AIDS Coalition to Unleash Power; founded in 1987 to protest the US government's inaction in preventing and treating HIV/AIDS. The group's media-savvy actions and graphics redefined activism.

ADONIS
One of the male physique magazines of the '50s that contained homoerotic pictures and found an audience among gay men; bonus: they were available at corner stores and newsstands.

BACKROOM
A space, often in the back of a gay bar, where men meet and engage in sexual activity; less common in United States these days, but still popular in Europe where they're often called "darkrooms."

BACKSTREET BOYS
One of the first in a parade of "boy bands" that dominated pop music in the 1990s; defined by all-American good looks and choreographed dance routines.

BIG BAND ERA
Large swing bands, such as those led by Benny Goodman and Glenn Miller, dominated popular music from 1935 to 1947 and routinely packed ballrooms and dance halls with lindy hopping and jitterbugging youth; eventually eclipsed by vocalists like Frank Sinatra and Ella Fitzgerald and, finally, rock-and-roll.

TYRA BANKS
A supermodel often seen in Victoria's Secret ads.

SANDRA BERNHARD
A queer comedian and satirist worshiped by certain gay men and women; also known for being Madonna's gal pal in the early '90s.

BOUGIE
Short for "bourgeois" which, according to *Merriam Webster*, means "of, relating to, or typical of the middle class"; connotes a preoccupation with material possessions and conformity.

BOYS STATE
The national leadership program for male high school juniors that teaches them about government and citizenship; founded in 1935 by the American Legion in response to fears about the spread of fascism.

BOYS IN THE BAND
The first Hollywood feature film to take an uncloseted look at homosexuality (1970). Based on the play by Matt Crowley, the camp classic focuses on a group of gay men gathered for a birthday party and reflects a slice of pre-Stonewall gay life.

ANITA BRYANT
In 1977, after a benign music career, the Christian fundamentalist, beauty queen and orange juice pitchwoman put her name and voice behind a campaign that repealed Miami/Dade County's gay anti-discrimination ordinance. Her "Save Our Children" campaign claimed that gay men, especially school teachers, were out to recruit boys and were unnatural. After Miami, she took her homophobic rant on the road, fighting gay rights ordinances across the country.

CARRIE
Stephen King's classic high school horror film (1977) starred Sissy Spacek as a telekinetic teen who eventually gets back at the bullies in her midst. On prom night, no less.

CB RADIO
Acronym: Citizen Band; "radio for the people" which allows anyone to communicate over short distances without a license; popular among families in the late 1970s during long car trips and still used by long-haul truckers.

CBS REPORTS
Hosted by Mike Wallace, the acclaimed documentary series gave Americans their first glimpse of openly gay people with its 1967 episode, "The Homosexuals." While it portrayed conventional thinking about homosexuality—that it was a psychiatric illness—it was also one of the first to present dissenting opinions.

CHICKEN
Slang: a young gay man.

CHRISTOPHER STREET
The Greenwich Village street has been an epicenter of gay male life in New York since World War II; also the site of Stonewall riots and the ensuing Gay Pride Marches. Queer nightlife still flourishes, but the street is less of a community focal point.

JOHN COLTRANE
A legendary American saxophonist known for innovative compositions and improvisations that revolutionized jazz music.

CONSCIOUSNESS-RAISING MODEL
Small-group discussions that were a major part of the feminist movement of the 1960s. While the model holds that the "personal was political," it also taps into a group's collective oppression. It was later applied to AIDS activism.

CRINOLINE
A stiff, cloth undergarment used to expand the gown worn over it; popular in the 1950s.

THE DEPRESSION
America's worst financial collapse began in 1929 and lasted through the 1930s, until World War II sparked production and revived the economy.

"DESPERADO"
A sad rock ballad by the Eagles; not romantic and therefore not typical prom fare.

SIMON DOONAN
The creative director of Barneys New York, a high-end clothing retailer; his elaborate Christmas window displays made him a style celebrity.

DRAG BALLS
Gay men dressed as women for what started as society balls in Harlem in the 1920s. The modern version, with its emphasis on competition, "realness" and groups called "houses," began popping up in the early '70s. Two decades later, Jennie Livingston's documentary *Paris Is Burning* introduced drag balls to the mainstream.

ELECTRIC COMPANY
Popular pre-teen television show from the '70s.

EVERYTHING YOU WANTED TO KNOW ABOUT SEX . . .
A best-selling how-to book that was one of the first to include a section on gay sex (1969); considered homophobic by some and scandalous by others.

FAG HAG
Slang: a woman who has many gay male friends.

FARRAH FAWCETT
All-American, blond bombshell from

the 1970s, who starred on TV's *Charlie's Angels*.

FIRE ISLAND
Since the 1940s, a popular queer summer destination near New York City.

F. SCOTT FITZGERALD
One of the most acclaimed authors of the twentieth century who wrote *The Great Gatsby* and *Tender Is the Night*; also known for his opulent lifestyle.

FORTY-FIVES
Records that rotate forty-five times per minute; also called "singles" because they usually hold a single song on each side; replaced by cassettes and compact discs.

FOX TROT
A ballroom dance that combines short and long, fast and slow steps.

AARON FRICKE
He sued his school's principal in 1980 to attend his prom with Paul Guilbert. By winning his case, Aaron set a precedent making it illegal to deny same-sex couples entry to school dances.

GAY ACTIVISTS ALLIANCE (GAA)
Founded in 1970 by break-away members of the more radical Gay Liberation Front (see below). GAA focused on changing laws through marches, pickets, political lobbying and dancing. And by hosting an intensely popular weekly dance at its firehouse headquarters in NYC, GAA reclaimed a piece of the gay social scene from bars like the Stonewall Inn, where gays routinely faced harassment from owners and raids by police.

GAY LIBERATION FRONT (GLF)
Formed days after the Stonewall riots by women and men who broke ranks with the conservative queer establishment epitomized by the Mattachine Society. The NYC group, informed by social ideals of the '60s, demanded an immediate end to homosexual persecution. By 1971, GLF expanded to more than eighty independent chapters across the US and abroad.

GAY RIGHTS ORDINANCES
Laws meant to protect queers from employment and housing discrimination; they were passed and, in some cases repealed, by voters in cities across the country in the early 1970s.

BARBARA GITTINGS
An early lesbian activist who joined the then-fledgling movement in 1958. An outspoken and articulate representative, she established the first East Coast chapter of the Daughters of Bilitis, the first known lesbian organization in the United States, and edited its pioneering magazine, *The Ladder*.

GRAND MARCH
A pre-prom tradition during which attendees parade in their finery often for public viewing; less common these days.

GRID
Acronym: Gay-Related Immune Deficiency; renamed AIDS in 1981.

PAUL GUILBERT
Attended prom with Aaron Fricke, who sued his principal to gain entry; Paul asked the school for permission to attend prom with a guy the previous year, but was turned down.

HADASSAH
An organization of Jewish women.

HARVEY MILK HIGH SCHOOL
The first public gay high school in the world; opened in the fall of 2003 in New York City.

HOHO®
A highly processed, chocolate snack cake in the tradition of Twinkies; introduced in 1967.

HORA
A Jewish folkdance in which a group moves in concentric circles; often performed at weddings and bar mitzvahs.

ROCK HUDSON
A closeted film actor who frequently co-starred opposite America's then-sweetheart Doris Day in the 1950s and 1960s; also appeared on *Dynasty*. In 1985, Hudson became one of the first celebrities to publicly acknowledge he was infected and dying of AIDS, helping to raise awareness while President Reagan still refused to utter the word in public.

JITTERBUG
An American swing dance popularized in the 1940s; consists of various two-step patterns embellished with twirls and sometimes acrobatic maneuvers.

KABBALAH
A medieval form of Jewish mysticism that has recently been popularized by Madonna et al.

KENT STATE
An Ohio university where, in 1971, National Guardsmen opened fire on students protesting the Vietnam War, killing four and wounding nine. Sparked widespread protests.

EVELYN CHAMPAGNE KING
The singer behind the 1977 disco classic "Shame."

LATKE
A fried potato appetizer much like a hash brown; usually eaten on Hannukah, a Jewish celebration also known as the "festival of lights."

LINDY HOP
One of the first swing dances that was popular in the 1930s; believed to be named after aviator Charles Lindbergh.

MATTACHINE SOCIETY
One of the first gay rights organizations in the United States. It was founded in 1950 by Harry Hay, but lost favor after Stonewall, when it became seen as too timid. Hay went on to start the Radical Faeries, a neo-pagan gay men's group.

HARVEY MILK
Elected to San Francisco's Board of Supervisors in 1977, Milk was one of the first openly gay people to hold public office in the United States. Became a gay icon after he was assassinated by a political rival.

GLENN MILLER
One of the most famous jazz musicians and band leaders of the Big Band era; his hits include "In the Mood" and "Chattanooga Choo Choo."

MY BEST FRIEND'S WEDDING
A 1997 romantic comedy staring Julia Roberts; features Rupert Everett as her handsome, best friend, who happens to be gay.

NEW YORK NATIVE
A gay newspaper that was one of the first to report extensively on the AIDS epidemic in the early 1980s.

NOW
Acronym: National Organization of Women; a feminist activist organization founded in 1966. NOW's goal is "to take action" to bring about equality for all women.

PARLIAMENT-FUNKADELIC
Two bands started, and later united, by George Clinton, who is considered one of the fathers of funk music. The groups helped create the new sound that fused rock, soul, psychedelia and gospel.

GLOSSARY

CONTINUED

PFLAG
Acronym: Parents, Families and Friends of Lesbians and Gays; started in 1972 by Jeanne Manford, who witnessed her son Morty being attacked at a gay rights demonstration on the local news. Her horror turned to outrage when she saw the police's failure to intervene.

PORKY'S
A trio of '80s movie about a group of high school students; is famous for its explicit sexual content and potty humor.

PRETTY IN PINK
A classic teen movie (1986) starring Molly Ringwald as a girl from the wrong side of the tracks who falls in love with a rich kid; it all comes to a boil at the prom.

PRINCESS PHONES
Sleek phones marketed more as decoration than a communication device.

PROVINCETOWN
A popular queer summer vacation spot on the tip of Cape Cod, Massachusetts.

RED-DIAPER BABY
Slang: toddler of communists/lefties.

ROLLER DISCO
Roller-skating to a disco beat; it was big in the late 1970s and early 1980s.

ETHEL ROSENBERG
She and her husband were executed in 1953 after being convicted of spying for the Soviet Union based on questionable evidence and by what many considered to be a prejudiced jury. Many believed they were killed because they refused to confess and name other members of the Communist Party.

SAGE
Acronym: Senior Action in a Gay Environment; the oldest and largest social service and advocacy organization dedicated to LGBT senior citizens started in 1977 in New York City; affiliate chapters in Florida, Nebraska, Rhode Island, Wisconsin, Washington D.C., Canada and Germany.

SALT-N-PEPA
With DJ Spinderella, this early female rap group scored in 1988 with "Push It"; the song is still a staple in clubs.

SAPPHIC
Of or relating to lesbianism; derived from Sappho, an ancient Greek poetess, who lived on the island of Lesbos and wrote love poems addressed to both women and men.

SEVENTY-EIGHTS
Originally, they were simply called "records." But after World War II, the typically ten-inch discs were renamed seventy-eights to distinguish them from new formats, such as forty-fives (which refers to the number of times they rotate per minute).

SISTER SOULJAH
A writer and rapper who gained worldwide attention in 1992 when would-be President Clinton condemned a comment she made during an interview as racist and extremist; many considered his repudiation an election-year political maneuver to appear more centrist and tougher on crime.

JERRY SPRINGER
The talk-show host who injected confrontation, controversy and chair throwing into the television genre; now the subject of an opera.

STONEWALL INN
Greenwich Village bar; site of the riots credited with launching the gay rights movement.

STONEWALL RIOTS
For three consecutive nights in the summer of 1969, queers tangled with the police after the largest gay bar in New York City was raided. This was one of the first times that gay men and women came together publicly to stand up for themselves. Considered by many to be the beginning of the modern gay rights movement, which relied more on confrontation and activism.

STUDENT STRIKES
In the late '60s and early '70s, college students across the country refused to go to class and took over campus buildings in protest of the Vietnam War and a variety of social issues and school policies.

SUGAR HILL GANG
The first hip hop group to find commercial success; their 1979 classic, "Rapper's Delight," introduced the US to hip hop and rap.

SUPERFRIENDS
A cartoon that brought together a cast of comic-book superheros; a staple of Saturday morning TV in the '70s.

HILARY SWANK
An actress who won an Academy Award® for her portrayal of Brandon Teena, a transgendered youth, who was murdered in 1994.

EMMETT TILL
A young black teen who was brutally murdered by two white men in 1955 in Mississippi. Emmett's crime: talking to a white women. (Apparently, he simply said, "Bye, bye.") The case drew national attention and mobilized the civil rights movement.

WEATHER UNDERGROUND
A radical group of largely upper-middle-class white kids which advocated the overthrow of the US government and, during the late '60s and '70s, executed a string of bombings, jailbreaks and riots; also known as the Weathermen.

THE WELL OF LONELINESS
A groundbreaking novel self-published by British author Radclyffe Hall in 1928. Even though it was initially banned and deemed obscene because its main character is a lesbian, her book went on to become an international best seller.

WHEAT PASTE
A technique by which posters are affixed to construction sites and other surfaces; a cost-efficient way for activists (and now corporations) to get their messages out on the street.

WILL & GRACE
An unapologetically queer sitcom featuring a gay man, Will and his best female friend Grace, who happens to be straight.

ZIONISM
A political movement—founded in 1897 in response to growing anti-Semitism—that worked to establish a Jewish state in the Middle East; after Israel was founded in 1948, Zionists focused on its defense.

I COULDN'T HAVE DONE IT WITHOUT YOU

DESIGNER
Jeff Ferzoco

DESIGN CONSULTANT
Martin Venezky

SOFT SKULL PRESS
Richard Nash
Sarah Palermo
Tennessee Jones

READERS
Dan Sacher
David Mills
David Thorpe
Ellen Umansky
John Garrison
Kaethe Fine
Larry Smith
Mimi O' Connor
Sam Zalutsky

TASK MASTERS
Piper Kerman
Jon Roemer

INTERNS
Dina Hoffer
Emily Lodish
Jenna Krajeski
Jenny Selig
Lynne Rosenberg
Temima Fruchter

AGENT
Tanya McKinnon,
Mary Evans Inc.

CONSTANT SUPPORT
Mom & Dad

WWW.GAYPROM.COM
Ted Rheingold & One Match Fire

SPECIAL THANKS
Alberto Orso
Alex Nowik
Andrew Copa, Vis Vitae
Andy Boyer
Barry Hoggard
Butchie
Colleen Werthmann
Craig Wright
Darleen & the kids at Gorilla Coffee
Dave Eggers
Doni Gewirtzman
Elana Koff
Eva Kolodner
Geoff Todebush
Hetrick-Martin Institute
Jim Sedlock
Joanna Hershon
Kerry Kennedy
LIGALY
Liz Schwartz
Maya Perez
Michael Boyer
Mimi Kaplan
New Leaf
SAGE
SAGE Queens
Sandi DuBowski
Seth McGinnis
Stephen Winter
Steven Melnick
Steven Manson
Everyone at Sullivan
The denizens of Versed
Vitali Rozynko

ANY UNINTENTIONAL OMISSIONS

AND, MOST ESPECIALLY, EVERYONE WHO SHARED THEIR STORIES

PUBLISHED BY SOFT SKULL PRESS
71 Bond Street, Brooklyn, NY 11217

Copyright © 2004 by David Boyer
Library of Congress Cataloging-in-Publication data for this book is
available from the Library of Congress.

ISBN 1-932360-24-7

Printed in China

IMAGE CREDITS
Many of the images came from the participants personal albums and scrap-
books. Where possible, the original photographer or illustrator is credited.

Cover and inside jacket illustrations: Jeff Ferzoco
Page 6: Luna Luis Ortiz/HMI
Page 10: Ed Haas
Page 11: James Arthur Wagner (protest pictures)
Page 13: Matt Meyer (graduation)
Page 18: Jay Drowns
Page 50: Eileen Callahan (collage)
Page 81: Theme illustrations by Steffan Schlarb
Page 88: Courtesy of Gerald Ford Library
Page 94: Courtesy of Catalina Video
Page 100: Courtesy of Colby College (IDs)
Page 101: Broadway Books (cover), Bruce Strong (photo)
Page 109: Joe Van Witsen
Page 114: Vincent Gagliostro
Page 121: Leigh McManus, STONEWALL Veterans' Association
Page 144: Courtesy of Minnesota Historical Society
Page 155: Cover art from a painting by Dan Nusinov